Bless My
GRANDCHILD

"If you have children of any age in your life, *Bless My Grandchild* is the book for you. Each of us has a role to play in mentoring children to 'pray without ceasing.' Julie Cragon's newest book provides an excellent prayer resource for all of life's experiences."

Bonnie Rodgers
CatholicTV

"This beautiful, blessed book will truly resonate with all grandparents, serving as an inspiration and guide as they pray for and with their grandchildren. The moment a child is conceived, a grandparent is born. Your loving response and prayers throughout their lives will help to encourage and support them in good times and in bad and serve as an example of how your faith has sustained you. You will want this book nearby—always."

Catherine Wiley
Founder of the Catholic Grandparents Association

"I love my grandchildren and have prayed for them since before they were born, but many times my prayers remain general and unfocused. In this beautiful book, filled with the love of God and the heartfelt affection of a grandparent, Julie Cragon offers a multitude of prayers for every stage and circumstance in the lives of our grandchildren. As an added gem, many of the prayers include intercession from various patron saints along with a brief description of their lives. This is a priceless resource that will bear fruit now and for eternity."

Bob Schuchts
Author of *Be Healed*
Founder of the John Paul II Healing Center

"This is a lovely resource full of prayers for just about every intention a grandparent could have, plus gentle saints to guide you as you pray."

Susie Lloyd
Author of *Yes, God!*

"This book puts beautiful words to all the longings of a grandparent's heart. There are prayers for every occasion, from the most joyous to the most difficult, and the author brings in the help of powerful patron saints. Like every Catholic grandparent, I need this book."

Mike Aquilina
Author of *A History of the Church in 100 Objects*

Bless My GRANDCHILD

A Catholic Prayer Book for Grandparents

Julie Cragon

Ave Maria Press AVE Notre Dame, Indiana

Founded in 1865, Ave Maria Press is a ministry of the United States Province of Holy Cross.

www.avemariapress.com

Paperback: ISBN-13 978-1-59471-933-2

E-book: ISBN-13 978-1-59471-934-9

Cover images © Getty Images.

Cover and text design by Brianna Dombo.

Printed and bound in the United States of America.

Library of Congress Cataloging-in-Publication Data
Names: Cragon, Julie, 1960- author.
Title: Bless my grandchild : a Catholic prayer book for grandparents / Julie Cragon.
Description: Notre Dame, Indiana : Ave Maria Press, 2020. | Summary: "This follow-up to Julie Cragon's bestseller, Bless My Child, combines original and traditional prayers and devotions designed to help readers place the joys and worries they experience as a grandparent back in the hands of God"-- Provided by publisher.
Identifiers: LCCN 2019046643 (print) | LCCN 2019046644 (ebook) | ISBN 9781594719332 (paperback) | ISBN 9781594719349 (ebook)
Subjects: LCSH: Grandparents--Prayers and devotions. | Catholic Church--Prayers and devotions.
Classification: LCC BV4845 .C73 2020 (print) | LCC BV4845 (ebook) | DDC 242/.8431--dc23
LC record available at https://lccn.loc.gov/2019046643
LC ebook record available at https://lccn.loc.gov/2019046644

Contents

Introduction xv

PRAYERS FOR BEFORE MY GRANDCHILD IS BORN

For an Unborn Grandchild (St. Gerard) 2

When Facing Struggles with Infertility 3

When Grieving a Miscarriage 4

For a New Mother (Mary) 5

For a New Father (St. Joseph) 6

For Twins or Multiple Births (St. Benedict and
     St. Scholastica) 7

PRAYERS FOR NEWBORN AND INFANT GRANDCHILDREN

For a Mother in Labor (St. Colette of Corbie) 10

For a Baby in Intensive Care (St. Nicholas) 11

In Celebration 12

For an Adopted Grandchild 13

For a Grandchild with Special Needs
     (Bl. Margaret of Castello) 14

For an Infant with Health Issues (St. Jude) 16

On the Death of My Tiny Grandchild 17

Prayers for Sacramental Graces

For a Child's Baptism (St. John the Baptist) 19

For a Grandchild Not Baptized 21

For First Reconciliation (St. Padre Pio) 22

For First Communion (Bl. Imelda Lambertini) 24

For Confirmation—Prayer to the Holy Spirit 25

For Altar Servers (St. John Berchmans) 26

For a Grandchild Getting Married 27

For the Marriage of My Grandchild's Parents 28

For Vocations (St. Teresa of Calcutta) 29

For the Anointing of the Sick 31

Prayers to Help My Grandchild
Grow in Virtue

A Morning Offering 33

For Grandchildren in Need of Guidance 34

For Faithfulness in Daily Duties 36

For Faith and Action (St. Elizabeth Ann Seton) 37

For Goodness 38

For Knowing True Beauty 39

For Holiness 40

For Joy 41

In Trials 42

For Humility 43

Against Harsh Judgments 44

For Living Kindness 45

For Living Love (Ven. Francois-Xavier
    Nguyễn Văn Thuận)......................... 46

For Living Mercy (St. Faustina Kowalska) 47

For Living Obedience (St. Ignatius of Loyola) 48

For Living Peace 49

For Living Persistence (St. Juan Diego) 51

For Living Purity (St. Agnes of Rome) 52

For Living Responsibility (Bl. Pier Giorgio
    Frassati) 53

For Strong Convictions 54

For Trust 55

For Charity 56

For Grandchildren in Need of Grandparents
    (Sts. Anne and Joachim) 57

Prayers for My Growing Grandchild

For Daily Care 59

For a Grandchild in Daycare 60

When a Grandchild Is Disciplined 61

For Playing with Others 62

For Sibling Bonds 63

For the First Day of School 64

As We Read Together 65

Prayers for Elementary and Middle School Years

To Reach Full Potential 67

To Make Good Daily Choices 68

For Commitment 69

For Safety in Playing Sports (Bl. Pier Giorgio
Frassati) 70

To Use Technology Wisely (St. Isidore of Seville) 71

To Cultivate Good Television Habits (St. Clare
of Assisi) 72

For Good Friendships 73

Against Negative Peer Pressure 74

For Courage (St. George of Lydda) 75

For Balance (St. John Paul II) 76

To Hear Jesus' Call 77

For Transitions 78

Prayers for Teenage Years

In High School (St. Raphael) 80

For a First Job Interview 81

For Gender Identity Issues 82

When a Grandchild Starts Dating 83

When a Grandchild Starts Driving
(St. Christopher) 84

For Choosing a College 85

On My Grandchild's Graduation 86

For a Grandchild Leaving Home 87

Against Wavering Faith (St. Monica) 88

For an Unwed Pregnancy 89

For a Serious Illness 90

For a Return to the Faith (St. Anthony of Padua) 91

When a Family Faces Divorce 93

When There Is a Death in the Family 94

PRAYERS FOR ADULT GRANDCHILDREN

Prayer for a Vocation (St. Alphonsus Liguori) 96

In Thanksgiving for the Single Life 97

A Marriage Blessing 98

When a Granddaughter Becomes a Mother 99

When a Grandson Becomes a Father 100

Prayer before an Adult Grandchild's Visit 101

Prayer after an Adult Grandchild's Visit 102

PRAYERS FOR SERIOUS NEEDS

For Acceptance of Imperfections 104

For Parents Fallen Away from the Faith 105

For a Struggling Marriage (St. Rita of Cascia) 106

For a Single Parent (St. Margaret of Cortona) 107

On the Loss of a Pet (St. Francis of Assisi) 108

For Those with Eating Disorders 109

For Those with Cancer (St. Peregrine Laziosi) 110

Before an Operation (Sts. Cosmas and Damian) 111

For Those with Anxiety and Depression

    (St. Dymphna) 112

On the Death of a Grandchild's Friend,

    with Faith 114

On the Death of a Grandchild's Friend,

    without Faith 115

On the Death of My Great-Grandchild 116

Traditional Prayers and Novenas

Introduction 118

Prayers

Act of Consecration to Our Lady of the

    Miraculous Medal 119

Act of Consecration to the Sacred Heart of Jesus 120

The Angelus 122

Anima Christi 124

Anima Christi for My Grandchild 125

Chaplet of Divine Mercy 126

Guardian Angel Prayer 128

Consecration of the Family 129

Mary, Undoer of Knots 131
Padre Pio Prayer for My Grandchild 132
Rosary for My Grandchild 133
St. Michael Prayer (Against Evil) 146
St. Patrick's Breastplate 147
St. Patrick's Breastplate for My Grandchild 148
From St. Teresa of Avila's Bookmark (For a
    Worried Grandchild) 150
St. Teresa of Avila Prayer 151
Stations of the Cross for My Grandchild 152

Novenas

A Nine-Day Novena for a Grandchild's Needs 160
Novena to Our Lady of Lourdes (For Healing) 165
Infant of Prague Novena of Childlike Confidence ... 166
Prayer to the Infant of Prague for My Grandchild ... 167
St. Andrew Novena (A Prayer to Conceive) 168
St. Jude Novena (For Medical Concerns) 169
St. Rita Novena (For Serious Illness) 170
St. Thérèse of the Child Jesus Novena 171

Acknowledgments 172

Introduction

The day my daughter called to tell me she was pregnant, I began praying for my grandchild. Not that I would be a good grandparent, but that this child would be healthy and happy and filled with the love of Christ and the love of her parents.

I can only imagine how St. Anne and St. Joachim felt when they found out their daughter was pregnant. Mary's explanation for her pregnancy—how an angel had visited her and declared that she would be "overshadowed" by the Holy Spirit to carry the Son of God into the world—must have stirred questions. And yet, I can imagine the great faith of St. Anne and St. Joachim to stand by and support their daughter during this most important time in history.

I am sure St. Anne and St. Joachim had concerns over what others might think and say about Mary and Joseph—concerns that would only grow over time as they realized the journey Mary and her family must take, the life they would lead, and the joys and the sorrows that lay before them. As a mother and a grandmother, I know that I will feel many of these things, too, and yet I will have the comfort of my faith and my prayers to see us all through.

One of the most important things we can do for our children and our grandchildren is to pray for them, to keep their names and their needs directly at the foot of the Cross. After all, this is where Jesus gave us his Mother, who continues to pray for us all. And so, as we slip into church and kneel before the tabernacle where Jesus dwells in his eucharistic presence, we implore our Lady to envelop us in her mantle. Oftentimes this is all we can do, all we need to do. Along with prayers to Jesus or to Jesus through Mary, we pray through the intercession of the saints. The lives of the saints show us that ordinary life is made extraordinary by faith, and their individual examples of virtue lead us to ask their help for specific needs—needs for ourselves and others.

Working in a Catholic bookstore, I am often asked to pray for the needs of the children and grandchildren of our customers and coworkers. Many of the prayers in this book are shared from my experiences of simply praying with others, thinking about the future of my own grandchild, and remembering the prayers lifted for other grandchildren in our extended family.

As children grow, we have less and less to teach them. As they reach adulthood, we know we have given them the tools to live well. They are moving on with their own families, and we must allow them to learn by living. Yet we must never stop praying for them, never stop being an example of prayer; and now we must also pray for their children, our grandchildren. We must pass on the power of prayer!

> "I would like to greet all grandmothers and grandfathers, thanking them for their valuable presence in families and for the new generations."
>
> —Pope Francis

Prayers for before My Grandchild Is Born

For an Unborn Grandchild
(St. Gerard)

St. Gerard, patron of expectant mothers,
watch over my unborn grandchild that she may be healthy
upon her birth and throughout her life.
May her tiny body be well nourished,
and may she feel the love we have for her even before she is
  born.
As my grandchild grows, may she remain close to God
all her life and follow his will.
St. Gerard, intercede for us to God, and bless my grandchild's
  parents
with an abundance of patience, wisdom, and perseverance.
May my grandchild be raised strong in faith and conviction
so that she may someday spend eternal life in heaven.
Amen.

ABOUT ST. GERARD MAJELLA (D. 1755)

One day while visiting a young family, Gerard dropped his
handkerchief in their home. As he was leaving, one of the girls
ran to return it. Gerard told her to keep it, saying, "You may
need it one day." He died shortly after that visit. Years later the
young girl, now married, was expected to die in childbirth.
Remembering the words of Gerard, she asked for his handkerchief from her drawer. When she held the cloth, the pain dis-
appeared, she was healed, and she gave birth to a healthy baby.
The story of the miracle spread quickly, and mothers began to
pray to St. Gerard for healthy births.

WHEN FACING STRUGGLES
WITH INFERTILITY

Lord, you know our every need.
You know I would love a grandchild, and
You know my daughter wants to have children,
yet has been unable to conceive.
Help her and her husband to accept what they cannot
   understand.
Help them to trust in your mercy and in your will for their lives.
In your great compassion,
give them the strength to persevere
in faith, in hope, and in love.
Strengthen their bond as they strive for understanding, allow-
   ing God
to guide them along the path he wants them to follow.
Amen.

If you wish to pray the St. Andrew Novena (A Prayer to Conceive), turn to page 168, under Traditional Prayers and Novenas.

WHEN GRIEVING A MISCARRIAGE

For I will restore your health; I will heal your
injuries.
—Jeremiah 30:17

Lord, I am devastated over the loss of my grandchild.

My heart just breaks, though I trust that she is safe in heaven
with you.

Comfort and heal her parents.

Of course, they are struggling to find understanding in this
time of deep sadness.

Help them—and all of us—to trust in you, to hold fast to our
faith.

Heal my daughter's body, her mind, and her soul.

Give her husband strength to support her as they grieve
together.

Give them the wisdom to rest in your loving arms and the
strength to persevere.

Restore her health, Lord. Heal their brokenness.

Amen.

FOR A NEW MOTHER
(MARY)

O Most Holy Mother of Jesus,
bless my daughter as she becomes a new mother.
Guide her in patience and understanding.
Fill her with your gifts of grace and peace.
Help her as she learns to love beyond understanding,
as she works to do God's will in her life.
Motherhood is filled with joys and sorrows.
May her joys far outweigh her sorrows.
Give her the strength and the wisdom to persevere.
Mary, may my daughter cling to you and find comfort
in being enfolded in your mantle.
Amen.

FOR A NEW FATHER
(ST. JOSEPH)

Good St. Joseph, patron of fathers and families,
bless my son as he welcomes his child.
Just as you were called upon to provide for Mary and Jesus,
bless him in his work to provide for his family.
Help him to be a man of integrity, loving, caring, and tender.
Teach him the importance of participating in his child's life,
of being there in his need, of unconditional love.
May he be an example of a true man of strength, faithful to God.
St. Joseph, stand with my son as he works in this life, and give
    him the proper tools to build his family of God.
Amen.

ABOUT ST. JOSEPH (FIRST CENTURY)

St. Joseph was the foster father of Jesus. An angel visited Joseph
in a dream, and he obeyed all that he was told. He took Mary
as his wife and moved his family according to the directions he
had been given from heaven. He did everything for the love of
his family and in obedience to the Lord.

FOR TWINS OR MULTIPLE BIRTHS
(ST. BENEDICT AND ST. SCHOLASTICA)

No trial has come to you but what is human.
God is faithful and will not let you be tried
beyond your strength.
—1 Corinthians 10:13

Lord, how blessed we are for our new grandchildren!
Bring them safely into the world together.
And as their parents' work is multiplied,
give them an equal measure of strength and patience,
and fill their hearts with an extra dose of joy and love.
St. Benedict and St. Scholastica, just as you supported one
    another in your vocations,
pray that our grandchildren may be a support to each other as
    they grow.
May their friendship and love be an example to others.
Lord, bless my grandchildren and their parents.
May they remain always faithful to you, and
may their lives imitate your great
Sts. Benedict and Scholastica.
Amen.

ABOUT ST. BENEDICT AND ST. SCHOLASTICA
(SIXTH CENTURY)

These sixth-century twins founded an order of Benedictine monks and nuns in Italy. Although Scholastica's order was cloistered, Benedict would meet his sister once a year for a visit. During their last day together, Benedict was ready to leave and Scholastica asked him to stay. As he reminded her that his rule required him to return to the monastery, a terrible storm arose, so bad that Benedict could not travel. The twins stayed up all night talking. Three days after Benedict returned home, he saw a dove ascending to the heavens and knew his sister had died. What a blessing and a miracle that a storm allowed them more time together!

Prayers for Newborn and Infant Grandchildren

FOR A MOTHER IN LABOR
(ST. COLETTE OF CORBIE)

St. Colette, pray for us today as my daughter labors
to bring her child into the world.
May her labor be quick and her joy complete.
As my grandchild enters this world, may she be healthy
and feel safe and secure and loved.
Today and every day, bless this sweet family, Lord,
that they may grow together in peace and love.
Amen.

ABOUT ST. COLETTE OF CORBIE (D. 1447)

Many miracles were attributed to this French abbess, who was
foundress of a reformed branch of the Poor Clares. In one
instance, St. Colette was traveling to Nice to meet Pope Benedict when she stopped by the home of a friend, whose wife
was in labor and was not expected to survive the birth. Colette
immediately went to the local church and prayed. When both
mother and child survived, the family credited St. Colette's
intercessory prayers. The child, christened Pierinne, later joined
the order founded by St. Colette. She became the elderly nun's
biographer and secretary, and she recorded other miracles
attributed to St. Colette as well. St. Colette is considered the
patroness of expectant mothers and sick children.

For a Baby in Intensive Care (St. Nicholas)

St. Nicholas, patron of children, watch over my tiny grandchild
as she struggles to fully develop. May she gain strength each
    day.
Bless her nurses in their intricate work.
Guide their hands and their hearts
as they work tirelessly for the lives of the babies in their care.
Intercede for us to Christ for the gift of a miracle.
We need the gifts of faith and trust.
Her parents need the light of hope.
St. Nicholas, guard my grandchild
and all other children who are fighting for their lives today.
Amen.

ABOUT ST. NICHOLAS (D. 343)

Although he is most popularly associated with the cultural icon
Santa Claus, St. Nicholas was a fourth-century bishop of Myra,
an ancient Greek city. He is best remembered in churches of
both East and West for his tender generosity to the poor and
vulnerable, as well as for his tireless defense of the Catholic
faith. He is the patron saint of children because of the multiple
stories involving his miraculous intervention to save the lives
of many in Myra. He helped a widower with dowries for his
daughters and saved the lives of three children who were going
to die at the hands of evil men.

In Celebration

Joy is very infectious; therefore, be always
full of joy.
—Mother Teresa

Lord, thank you for my beautiful grandchild.
She fills our family with joy.
As I learn my place in her life,
help me to cherish each moment.
Her mere presence is a gift.
As she makes her way in this life,
may she feel my support.
If she stumbles, may she know that I am here for her.
I am grateful.
Words cannot express the joy she brings.
Lord, thank you.
Amen.

For an Adopted Grandchild

All things are possible for God.
—Mark 10:27

Lord, my children have brought this beautiful grandchild
into our lives through adoption.
You have heard and answered our prayers.
Help her to feel comfortable and loved.
Bless us all with a gentle transition.
As she finds her way in our family,
may she learn the ways of your love, Lord,
an unconditional love that sees differences and struggles,
but perseveres even through the hard times.
Open our hearts to one another, and give us patience.
Lord, hold my precious grandchild gently in your loving care
today and every day. Give her peace.
Amen.

FOR A GRANDCHILD
WITH SPECIAL NEEDS
(BL. MARGARET OF CASTELLO)

Bl. Margaret, you know what it is
to be different from other children. Intercede for us so
that my precious grandchild may be treated with patience and
understanding.
Together we will face difficult challenges;
pray for us, that we will work together to help him become
the person God created him to be.
In loving him, may we learn how much God loves us.
In guiding him, may we understand his patience.
We give thanks for his strong will and his loving heart.
Pray for us, dear Margaret, that we might always be thankful
for the gift of his life, so perfect in the eyes of Christ.
Bl. Margaret, help those he encounters to love him
as much as we love him.
Amen.

ABOUT BL. MARGARET OF CASTELLO
(D. 1320)

Born blind and with several physical difficulties, this future
Dominican sister was abandoned by her parents at the age of
six after they took her to a shrine for healing, and realized she
would not be healed. A woman in the town found her and
took her home, where Margaret flourished and soon became

a favorite of the city. She worked with the sick and spent time with those who were lonely and grieving. When she died, she was buried inside the town church, and the entire town attended her funeral.

For an Infant with Health Issues (St. Jude)

St. Jude, intercede for us for our grandchild.
Her situation seems desperate.
Watch over her as she struggles to fully develop.
Ask God to help her to gain strength daily so that she may grow to be healthy in mind and body and spirit.
Bless the nurses and doctors who care for her, and guide their hands.
She needs the gift of a miracle, and we need the gifts of faith and trust.
Help us as we pray for her healing.
Amen.

If you wish to pray the St. Jude Novena, turn to page 169 in Traditional Prayers and Novenas.

ABOUT ST. JUDE THE APOSTLE (D. 70)

St. Jude is the patron saint of hope and impossible causes, and he was one of the original twelve followers of Christ. He is the brother of James the Less, not to be confused with Judas Iscariot. It is partly because of the similarity of their names that St. Jude became the patron of lost causes—it was thought that few invoked his intercession, so he had time for the really tough assignments!

ON THE DEATH OF
MY TINY GRANDCHILD

Lord, I just need time to grieve. I need to cry.

My poor son and daughter-in-law—their loss is devastating.

Help me to be a good example of faith, someone they can rely on for comfort. Nothing I can say or do will make this easier. This is between you and them.

We do not know the reasons why. Help us to cling to one another as family.

Help me to listen—just listen and be present.

Amen.

Prayers for Sacramental Graces

For a Child's Baptism
(St. John the Baptist)

Then Jesus came from Galilee to John at the
Jordan to be baptized by him. John tried to
prevent him, saying, "I need to be baptized
by you, and yet you are coming to me?" Jesus
said to him in reply, "Allow it now, for thus
it is fitting for us to fulfill all righteousness."
Then he allowed him.

—Matthew 3:13–15

St. John the Baptist, your entire life was spent pointing others
to Christ.
Pray for my grandchild today, that he will live for Jesus too.
And just as you were called to baptize Jesus,
so we are called to witness to the baptism of our grandchild.
May he be cleansed with the waters of life and anointed with
chrism,
that he may live always as a member of the Body of Christ.
May the flame of Christ be the light for his life so
that he may follow the teachings of the Church.
As he wears the white garment of purity,
may he grow each day to be chaste in word and deed.
And may his godparents truly support
his commitment to the Catholic Church.
St. John, you decreased so that others could see Christ.
Intercede for my grandchild,

that he may continually see Christ in his life and an increase
in his faith.
Amen.

ABOUT ST. JOHN THE BAPTIST (FIRST CENTURY)

St. John was a cousin of Jesus and a herald of Jesus' public ministry from the time their mothers were still carrying them in the womb (see Luke 1:39–56). Although St. John died before Jesus (see Mark 6:17–29), he did fulfill an important mission. God called him to baptize Jesus in the Jordan River, where Jesus instituted the Church's Sacrament of Baptism.

FOR A GRANDCHILD NOT BAPTIZED

A voice came from the heavens, saying,
"This is my beloved Son, with whom
I am well pleased."
—Matthew 3:17

Lord, even you were baptized by St. John the Baptist!
You know that I desire baptism for my grandchild.
But this is between you and her parents.
Fill them with the grace to choose Baptism for their children.
Strengthen them in your Spirit.
I will continue to pray, and to trust, and to encourage,
until at last she receives the sacrament of Baptism.
Father, I want you to be "well pleased" with my grandchild.
Help me to be faithful so that one day she may become
part of the family of God.
Amen.

FOR FIRST RECONCILIATION
(ST. PADRE PIO)

My grandchild is celebrating his First Reconciliation!
Padre Pio, intercede for him so that he makes a good confession.
May he understand the gift of forgiveness.
May he feel the love and mercy of Christ
so that he in turn can show love and mercy to others.
May the priest help him to love the sacrament
so that he will return often and know the importance of frequent confession.
Padre Pio, as you guided so many through confession to be purified,
guide my grandchild so that he may receive the Body and Blood of Christ
with a pure heart and so that he may strive to live free from the weight of sin.
Amen.

ABOUT ST. PADRE PIO OF PIETRELCINA (D. 1968)

St. Padre Pio was a Capuchin Franciscan friar and confessor. At the time of his death, Pio's order estimated that the friar had heard twenty-five thousand confessions a year. It is believed that he could "read souls," reminding penitents of the sins they forgot to confess! Many miracles are attributed to the intercession of St. Pio as well as the return of many back to the Church. He is pictured wearing gloves because his body bore the wounds of Christ, the stigmata. He is a great saint to intercede for the holiness of our children and grandchildren—and for ourselves as well.

FOR FIRST COMMUNION
(BL. IMELDA LAMBERTINI)

Bl. Imelda, you had a deep desire to receive
Jesus in the Eucharist at an early age.
My grandchild has that same deep desire today for his First
  Communion.
May he continue this feeling throughout his life.
He is quiet and peaceful and serious.
Obviously full of respect and reverence,
my grandchild is a beautiful example to his friends and family.
May today only increase his desire to draw closer to Christ.
Amen.

ABOUT BL. IMELDA LAMBERTINI (D. 1333)

Born in Italy, Bl. Imelda desired to receive Communion at a
young age. Even after joining a Dominican convent at the age of
nine, she was considered too young, since at that time children
did not receive Jesus in the Eucharist until they were twelve
years old!

One day as Imelda prayed before the tabernacle, the sisters
in the chapel could see a host above her head. The priest also
saw the host and gave Imelda the Eucharist. Full of joy, Imelda
died the next day. She is the patroness of first communicants.

FOR CONFIRMATION—
PRAYER TO THE HOLY SPIRIT

Confirmation deepens our baptismal life
that calls us to be missionary witnesses to
Jesus Christ in our families, neighborhoods,
society and the world.
—*United States Catholic Catechism for Adults*

Come Holy Spirit, fill my grandchild with your gifts
of wisdom, understanding, counsel, fortitude,
knowledge, piety, and fear of the Lord.
Be her helper and her guide.
Enkindle in her the fire of your love,
that she may be a source of love to others.
Bless her sponsor so that they may stay close
and she may guide and support my grandchild especially
    through times of trial.
As my grandchild accepts this deeper responsibility to her bap-
    tismal promises,
may she be strengthened as a Christlike witness
to those she meets each day.
Amen.

FOR ALTAR SERVERS
(ST. JOHN BERCHMANS)

St. John Berchmans, the first time you served on the altar
you were blessed with a deep love to assist at Mass daily.
Intercede for my grandchild as he serves,
that he may experience that same deep love.
My heart is full as I watch him assist the priest.
May he love the Mass all his life as much as he loves it today.
May he choose to serve frequently,
and draw closer to Christ each time he is on the altar.
Amen.

ABOUT ST. JOHN BERCHMANS (D. 1621)

St. John Berchmans, a Jesuit scholastic, is the patron saint of
altar servers. From a young age he served Mass, and from the
first moment on the altar he loved to serve. He often volun-
teered to serve more than one Mass per day. He became a good
priest and drew others closer to Christ by his example of simple
holiness.

FOR A GRANDCHILD
GETTING MARRIED

For this reason a man shall leave [his] father
and [his] mother and be joined to his wife,
and the two shall become one flesh.

—Ephesians 5:31

Lord, watch over this couple as they prepare
for the sacrament of marriage.
Help them to keep you as the center of their minds and their
hearts
as they grow in love for you and for each another.
May they learn to pray as a couple, coming to you for strength
in good times and in hard times, in their joys and in their
sorrows.
May they be open to children, as they grow in their love.
And may they work as one, with you, Lord,
to be an example of unity and peace in their community.
Bless these two and all they do, today and every day of their
lives.
Amen.

For the Marriage
of My Grandchild's Parents

Again, amen, I say to you, if two of you agree
on earth about anything for which they are
to pray, it shall be granted to them by my
heavenly Father. For where two or three are
gathered together in my name, there am I in
the midst of them.

—Matthew 18:19–20

Lord, bless this couple, my grandchild's parents.
May they be strong examples of family life.
May they continue to love and to respect one another.
May they share their gift of love,
through prayer for others and through their example of a happy,
    healthy relationship.
May their marriage and their love for family be an example to
    others.
May my grandchild grow up with a living example of a good
    Christian marriage,
so that one day she will want to continue this bond of love with
    her own family.
May this circle be unbroken, Lord, as we place our trust in you.
Amen.

For Vocations
(St. Teresa of Calcutta)

> Our vocation is nothing else but to belong to
> Christ. The work that we do is only a means
> to put our love for Christ into living action.
> —St. Teresa of Calcutta

St. Teresa, you experienced your vocational "call within a call"
and understood that there is much work to be done in this
   world.
We need to serve one another. We need to love and care for
   others.
We need to put our love for the living Christ into action.
As my grandchild discerns a vocation to religious life,
may he grow deeper in spiritual love and in piety.
May he humble himself to serve others,
to be the hands and the feet and the heart of Christ
that we so terribly need in this world.
May he gain wisdom in truth, and as he follows his calling,
may he find joy and peace.
St. Teresa, you worked tirelessly in service to others.
Pray for my grandchild, that he will learn
to do all for the greater glory of God.
Amen.

ABOUT ST. TERESA OF CALCUTTA (D. 1997)

Mother Teresa founded the Missionaries of Charity after obeying God's call to serve the poorest of the poor. These religious sisters manage homes for the sick and dying, as well as running soup kitchens, clinics, and children's programs throughout the world. She is probably best known for her work in the slums of India.

For the Anointing of the Sick

> Is anyone among you sick? He should summon the presbyters of the church, and they should pray over him and anoint [him] with oil in the name of the Lord, and the prayer of faith will save the sick person, and the Lord will raise him up. If he has committed any sins, he will be forgiven.
>
> —James 5:14–15

Lord Jesus, the one you love, my grandchild, is sick. We feel
    so helpless.
Come with your healing touch.
Send the comforting balm of your Spirit.
As he is anointed with the holy chrism,
touch his body and heal him, according to your will.
Give the doctors wisdom, and give us strength
to endure what we must with faith.
Jesus, we trust in you.
Amen.

Prayers to Help My Grandchild Grow in Virtue

A Morning Offering

For he commands his angels with regard to
you, to guard you wherever you go.
—Psalm 91:11

Lord, bless my grandchild as he rises.
May the angels watch over him and protect him.
May they lead him in the ways of love.
May he be blessed with an unselfish spirit,
a heart that cares for others.
May his hands be of service, and may he lead others in the way
of truth.
May he be an example of kindness to all who cross his path.
May he be filled with wisdom and understanding,
and may he be a reflection of your love.
O Lord, each day may the wings of the angels enfold him
and guide him down the road that leads directly back to you.
Amen.

For Grandchildren in Need of Guidance

Children, obey your parents [in the Lord],
for this is right. "Honor your father and
mother." This is the first commandment
with a promise, "that it may go well with you
and that you may have a long life on earth."
Fathers, do not provoke your children to
anger, but bring them up with the training
and instruction of the Lord.

—Ephesians 6:1–4

Lord, my heart feels as if it could burst wide open.
I love my grandchild and want her to grow in goodness.
And yet she can be so stubborn and say things that are hurtful.
She often tunes me out as she plays on her phone.
How can I guide her along the right path?
I want my grandchild to know and love you.
And I want her to know how much I love her too.
So help me, Lord.
Set a watch over my mouth, to stifle harsh words and impatient
    outbursts.
Help me to remember to model kindness and patience with
    her parents too.
And keep me from doing and saying too much. Help me to
    support her.

Teach me how to be a godly grandparent; speak to me through
　　your Word.
I have sown the seed the best I can.
Now I trust you to help that seed to grow in her parents,
so that they will train my grandchild to know and love you.
Each day put upon my heart the prayers they need most.
Give us all the grace to follow you and the wisdom
to call upon your Holy Spirit for all we need.
Amen.

For Faithfulness in Daily Duties

Great holiness consists in carrying out the
little duties of each moment.
—St. Josemaría Escrivá

Lord, bless my sweet grandchild as he learns responsibility.
Help him to see that daily chores, done joyfully
and with good intention, can gain us heaven.
Help him to understand the importance of working as a family.
These moments of togetherness are moments of holiness.
Give us strength, Lord, so that all we do may reflect
your goodness, your kindness, and your glory.
Amen.

ABOUT ST. JOSEMARÍA ESCRIVÁ (D. 1975)

St. Josemaría Escrivá, the founder of Opus Dei, taught that the ordinary activities of daily life are our path to holiness. His life was an example of following the will of God naturally. He is also the patron saint of diabetes, having had type 1 diabetes most of his life.

FOR FAITH AND ACTION
(ST. ELIZABETH ANN SETON)

God has given me a great deal to do and I
have always and hope always to prefer his
will to every wish of my own.
—St. Elizabeth Ann Seton

St. Elizabeth, you are a beautiful example of
listening for God's will in your life and acting accordingly.
Intercede for my grandchild,
that she may be open to all God wants in her life and
that she may unselfishly follow his will.
Help her to cling to the teachings of the Church and the power
of the Eucharist.
May my grandchild's faith be a source of strength
so that she can make a difference in the lives of others.
Amen.

ABOUT ST. ELIZABETH ANN SETON (D. 1821)

St. Elizabeth Ann Seton lost both her mother and her husband
while she was young, yet she put all her faith and trust in the
will of God. She started the first free Catholic school in America, opened two orphanages, and founded the Sisters of Charity
of St. Joseph. She was a hardworking woman of great faith and
incredible perseverance. May all our grandchildren have a heart
like hers.

FOR GOODNESS

Indeed, goodness and mercy will pursue
me all the days of my life; I will dwell in the
house of the LORD for endless days.
—Psalm 23:6

Lord, may goodness and mercy pursue my grandchild
as she grows into all she is capable of becoming.
May her thoughts and her words and her deeds
be filled with kindness.
May she always seek the best in herself and others.
May she always stay close to you and
be an example of good and merciful leadership.
May she help to bring others closer to you in this life,
that we may all someday live with you for eternity.
Amen.

FOR KNOWING TRUE BEAUTY

> God, by looking within himself, is impassioned for the beauty of his creature and, as if transported by love, he created man in his own image and likeness.
> —St. Catherine of Siena

Lord, you are the source of our beauty.
As I watch my beautiful grandchild grow,
I pray that she will know you and understand the meaning of true beauty.
How wonderfully she is made in your image!
What I see in her is surely the beauty of God.
I pray that she will understand and appreciate your gifts to her and
the all-encompassing love you have for each of us.
Lord, may my grandchild spread your beauty and
your love to all those around her.
Amen.

For Holiness

As he who called you is holy, be holy yourselves in every aspect of your conduct, for it
is written, "Be holy because I am holy."
—1 Peter 1:15–16

Lord, we are all called to be holy,
and yet, in the world today,
holiness seems to be more the exception than the norm.
Bless my grandchild with the desire to persevere
toward holiness, completing her Christian duties with love,
doing the small tasks well.
Give her the daily grace to live a full Christian life and
to persevere toward the ultimate reward of heaven.
Help her to be the exception and to imitate you.
Amen.

FOR JOY

For to the one who pleases God, he gives
wisdom and knowledge and joy.
—Ecclesiastes 2:26

Lord, I know it is your great pleasure
when we are happy and joyful.
This is the wish I have for my grandchild: complete joy.
And in return, I'd like him to spread joy
to his family and friends and community.
This life needs more joy-filled people.
Help my grandchild to cast aside
his fears and doubts and anxieties and
find simple joy.
Amen.

IN TRIALS

Consider it all joy, my brothers, when you
encounter various trials, for you know
that the testing of your faith produces
perseverance.

—James 1:2–3

Lord, our faith is tested every day.
This is the way of the world.
People try to fill us with doubt and despair.
They try to convince us that we are left on our own
to make it through the tough parts of life.
Lord, when my grandchild is pushed toward doubt,
let him know you are here.
When he struggles in despair,
help him to feel your presence.
Enlighten his understanding
so that as he perseveres through the trials in this world,
he will receive the amazing gifts of your grace and your promise.
Amen.

For Humility

For everyone who exalts himself will be
humbled, but the one who humbles himself
will be exalted.

—Luke 14:11

Lord, the temptation is always before us
to put ourselves first, to make ourselves "number one."
Help my grandchild not to follow the ways of the world.
May he put you first in his life, Lord, and
his friends and others before himself.
Out of simple kindness, may he humble himself
as you humbled yourself for each one of us.
May he follow your will for his life,
listening and believing,
knowing that through you he will be saved.
Amen.

Against Harsh Judgments

In order not to be judged hereafter, it is
equally necessary that we should refrain
from judging others, and that we should be
careful to judge ourselves.
—St. Francis de Sales

Lord, at times we criticize others harshly,
attributing bad motives to someone else
in order to make ourselves look better.
And yet, only you know what is truly on our hearts.
Help my grandchild to leave such things in your hands,
knowing that you alone are the judge of all.
Teach him to control his tongue and
to open his heart to love others unconditionally.
When someone is doing something to harm himself or others,
give him wisdom to encourage that person in love,
correcting his error with humility
in order to help him choose a better path.
Help us all to live in love.
Amen.

ABOUT ST. FRANCIS DE SALES (D. 1622)

St. Francis de Sales was a great preacher and writer. His most
famous work, *Introduction to the Devout Life*, stresses living the
spiritual life by loving God and one another, even over doing
acts of penance.

For Living Kindness

Let there be kindness in your face, in your
eyes, in your smile, in the warmth of your
greeting. Always have a cheerful smile. Don't
only give your care, but give your heart as
well.

—St. Teresa of Calcutta

Jesus, a kind heart is rare and full of virtue.
Teach my grandchild to be kind.
A kind soul goes beyond the norm.
Teach my grandchild to go beyond.
A kind act reaches past the immediate.
Teach my grandchild to stretch herself.
A kind person thinks beyond themselves.
Teach my grandchild to put others first.
Lord, may my grandchild show kindness
in her face, in her eyes, in her smile, in her words, and in her
    actions.
Help her to possess true kindness.
Amen.

FOR LIVING LOVE
(VEN. FRANCOIS-XAVIER
NGUYỄN VĂN THUẬN)

Once Mother Teresa of Calcutta wrote me,
"What is important is not how many actions
we perform, but the intensity of love that we
put into each action."
—Ven. Francois-Xavier Nguyễn Văn Thuận

Lord, we know that all good comes to those who love you.
I pray that my grandchild will learn to love you with her whole
heart
so that she can love others through her words and actions
with that same intensity. Help her to live in love.
You loved us so much that, at your death,
your side was opened to reveal your Sacred Heart to the world.
Help my grandchild to open her heart to those she meets,
to love genuinely and to be loved in return.
Amen.

ABOUT VEN. FRANCOIS-XAVIER
NGUYỄN VĂN THUẬN

Ven. Francois-Xavier Nguyễn Văn Thuận was held prisoner in
a communist reeducation camp for thirteen years. Compiled
from the smuggled notes he sent to friends, his story *The Road
of Hope* tells of his incredible faith and intense love during his
life of imprisonment and torture.

FOR LIVING MERCY
(ST. FAUSTINA KOWALSKA)

St. Faustina, apostle of Divine Mercy,
intercede for my grandchild so that she may share Jesus' mercy.
Help her not to hold grudges.
Help her not to share gossip.
Help her to be merciful to her family and her friends,
especially those difficult to get along with.
May she show mercy to the less fortunate and
get involved in acts of mercy toward the less privileged, the
    poor, and the weak.
May the Lord forgive us in his great mercy and
help us all to be examples of forgiveness to others.
Amen.

ABOUT ST. FAUSTINA KOWALSKA (D. 1938)

St. Faustina was a Polish sister of the Blessed Sacrament. Jesus
appeared to her beginning in 1931 and asked her to have an
image made of him as he appeared, with the signature "Jesus
I Trust in You." He also asked that the image be blessed on the
Sunday after Easter, now celebrated as Divine Mercy Sunday.
Her conversations with Jesus can be found in the *Diary of Saint
Maria Faustina Kowalska: Divine Mercy in My Soul.*

*If you wish to pray the Chaplet of Divine Mercy, turn to page 126
under Traditional Prayers and Novenas.*

For Living Obedience
(St. Ignatius of Loyola)

It is not hard to obey when we love the one
whom we obey.
—St. Ignatius of Loyola

Lord, I pray that my grandchild will follow your commandments.
Of all the rules she is asked to follow throughout her life,
these are the most important
to help her discern right from wrong and to grow in goodness.
Obeying you is the greatest challenge with the greatest reward.
Bless her with a desire for obedience,
that she may flourish in grace and peace,
staying close to you in faith and love.
Amen.

ABOUT ST. IGNATIUS OF LOYOLA (D. 1556)

St. Ignatius of Loyola cofounded the Society of Jesus (the Jesuits) and is best known for his *Spiritual Exercises*. As the first superior of the Jesuits, Ignatius sent missionaries all over Europe to open schools, colleges, and seminaries. In the Jesuit *Constitutions*, St. Ignatius stressed obedience to the pope and to the Church hierarchy.

For Living Peace

Lord, make me an instrument of your peace:
where there is hatred, let me sow love;
where there is injury, pardon;
where there is doubt, faith;
where there is despair, hope;
where there is darkness, light;
where there is sadness, joy;
O divine Master, grant that I may not so
much seek
to be consoled as to console,
to be understood as to understand,
to be loved as to love.
For it is in giving that we receive,
it is in pardoning that we are pardoned,
and it is in dying that we are born to eternal
life.
—Hymn attributed to St. Francis of Assisi

Lord, make my grandchild an instrument of your peace.
Where there is hatred, let him show love.
Where others are injured, physically, mentally, and spiritually,
let him help them with compassion.
Where there is self-doubt, Lord, may he hold fast to the faith.
Where there is darkness and despair, may he spread the light
of hope,
and where he finds sadness, may he share joy.

O divine Master, grant that my grandchild may not so much
   seek
to be consoled as to console,
to be understood as to understand,
to be loved as to love.
For it is in giving that he will receive,
it is in forgiving that he will be forgiven,
and it is in dying to self that he will gain eternal life with you.
Amen.

Bless My Grandchild

FOR LIVING PERSISTENCE
(ST. JUAN DIEGO)

St. Juan Diego, just as you persisted in going to Mass
despite having to walk a long distance,
please pray for my grandchild to be persistent in her faith.
Just as you continued to visit the bishop
to share the appearance of Our Lady,
may my grandchild remain persistent in her journey
to keep and spread the faith.
May she ask for Our Lady's help,
continually coming to the Lord in prayer, just as you did.
May she always rely upon
your friendship, Our Lady's love, and God's mercy.
Amen.

ABOUT ST. JUAN DIEGO (D. 1548)

St. Juan Diego was taking the long walk to Mass when Our
Lady appeared to him in Guadalupe, Mexico, and told him to
ask the bishop to build a church. The bishop did not believe
that Our Lady had appeared to Juan Diego, and so Our Lady
worked a miracle for Juan Diego—creating her image in his
cloak (*tilma*). The bishop was finally convinced, the shrine was
built, and the *tilma* is still displayed in the shrine that was built
to venerate Our Lady of Guadalupe. Juan Diego is an example
of an ordinary person who exhibited extraordinary love for
Our Lady and her Son.

FOR LIVING PURITY
(ST. AGNES OF ROME)

St. Agnes, patron saint of purity,
pray that my grandchild will remain chaste in body, mind, and
    heart.
Keep her from harm.
Guide her choices, and help her not to give in to temptation.
Pray that she will be mindful of how she dresses and how she
    acts.
Help her to be respectful and to command respect.
St. Agnes, pray that my grandchild will embrace a life of chastity.
Amen.

ABOUT ST. AGNES OF ROME (D. 304)

In sacred art St. Agnes is depicted with a lamb. Her name comes
from the Latin for "lamb," *agnus*, which also means "pure." She
was a beautiful young girl who refused the pursuit of many
men. She dedicated herself to God, and many miracles occurred
because of her example of holiness.

FOR LIVING RESPONSIBILITY
(BL. PIER GIORGIO FRASSATI)

Dear Bl. Pier Giorgio, you took responsibility
for many of the people you met in your short life,
as well as for yourself and your family.
You brought friends to prayer,
you took medicine to the sick, and
you sacrificed so others could have the basics of life.
Intercede for my grandchild
so that he will make responsible choices
with his friends and those in his community.
Help him to own his behavior,
to do what is right for his family and his friends.
Give him the grace to act justly and
to walk in the light of the ever-present Christ.
Amen.

ABOUT BL. PIER GIORGIO FRASSATI (D. 1925)

Bl. Pier Giorgio Frassati was an Italian who at a very young age
gave his shoes to a child in need and who continued this generous lifestyle until his death at age twenty-four. St. John Paul II
referred to him as the "Man of the Eight Beatitudes" because of
his continual giving nature. He was strong in sports, in friendships, and in his spiritual life. He loved mountain climbing, ski-
ing, and swimming and found great joy in life with his friends.

FOR STRONG CONVICTIONS

May the LORD keep watch between you and
me when we are out of each other's sight.
—Genesis 31:49

Dear Lord, you are our strength and our salvation.
To you we come for help in this world of chaos and uncertainty,
a world that has lost the Spirit of truth.
Watch over my grandchild, so easily led astray
by options that can harm his soul.
Help his family to instill your truth, your love,
your hope, and your mercy.
Help him to hold fast to his beliefs,
especially when it is most difficult to see the truth.
Give him strength in his convictions.
Amen.

FOR TRUST

When a soul approaches me with trust, I fill
it with such an abundance of graces that it
cannot contain them within itself, but radi-
ates them to other souls.
                                    —St. Faustina Kowalska

Dear Jesus, pour out your mercy on my grandchild
so that she may have the confidence to approach you with trust.
May she always feel free to talk to you, to confide in you,
to ask for the abundant graces you want to bestow upon her.
May she radiate your love and your mercy and your peace.
Fill her with all she needs to trust in your infinite goodness.
Jesus, we trust in you.
Amen.

FOR CHARITY

When you have finished your work, do your
brother's, helping him, for the sake of Christ.
With such finesse and naturalness that no
one—not even he—will realize that you are
doing more than in justice you ought. This,
indeed, is virtue befitting a son of God.
—St. Josemaría Escrivá

Lord, give my grandchild a kind and loving heart.
Help him to see the needs of others before his own.
May he grow in charity daily,
acting as your hands and your feet on earth,
expecting nothing in payment for his good deeds.
It is not easy doing thankless jobs,
giving without receiving, going beyond what we are asked.
Give my grandchild the grace he needs, Lord,
to do small acts with great charity.
May his rewards be great in heaven.
Amen.

For Grandchildren in Need of Grandparents (Sts. Anne and Joachim)

Lord, today I think of children all over the world
who have no grandparents to pray for them.
May all grandchildren be loved and cared for.
May they all be clothed and fed.
May they all know your love and your peace.
In this age, when children are exposed to the harsh realities
    of life,
help us to work together to protect them, to nourish them, to
    love them all.
Just as St. Anne and St. Joachim once held you, nourished you,
    and loved you,
please draw these precious children to your Sacred Heart, and
let them know a grandparent's love.
Amen.

About Sts. Anne and Joachim
(First Century)

Sts. Anne and Joachim are the parents of Mary, the Mother of God, and therefore the grandparents of Jesus. As this couple grew together in love for one another, they also grieved for their inability to conceive a child. They are most often celebrated together as a couple because it was together that they joined into fasting and prayer until that glorious day when an angel revealed that the Lord had blessed Anne to give birth to the Mother of our Savior.

Prayers for My Growing Grandchild

FOR DAILY CARE

Dear Jesus, watch over this grandchild as she grows.
As she is cared for with tender hands, may she in turn be tender.
As she is loved with sincere hearts, may she open her heart to
    others.
As she is helped to take first steps, may she learn to walk in
    your ways.
May she carry your message of love in her heart and
offer it to others as she grows
so that your peace may grow in the world.
Amen.

For a Grandchild in Daycare

Lord, I wish I could always be with my grandchild,
but since I cannot, I pray that you will watch over her.
Send her guardian angel to protect her always.
Bless the hands that hold her
so she will feel loved throughout the day
while her parents are working.
Help her to play well with others and
learn to get along with everyone.
Bless her teachers with patience and love and understanding.
Amen.

*If you wish to pray the Guardian Angel Prayer, turn to page 128
under Traditional Prayers and Novenas.*

WHEN A GRANDCHILD
IS DISCIPLINED

O Lord, help my grandchild's parents
as they discipline their child.
May he accept responsibility for his actions and
learn from his punishment.
Help my grandchild to understand
that discipline from his parents or grandparents at home
helps him know how to act in public.
Though it is sometimes unpleasant,
children need to learn from those who love them the most.
Help us, Lord, and help my grandchild as we navigate this life
together.
Amen.

For Playing with Others

Dear Lord, my grandchild is going to a friend's house.
Help him to be polite.
Help him to share with his friends and
to understand if others do not share with him.
Help him to have good manners,
and protect him until he returns home.
Amen.

FOR SIBLING BONDS

Dear Lord, as this family grows,
help my grandchildren to learn
to enjoy each other and to play well together.
When conflicts arise, help them to learn to forgive quickly.
May my grandchildren love one another, and
may their bond grow deeper as they grow.
May they know how fortunate they are
to share common needs and common goals.
Lord, bless my grandchildren.
Amen.

FOR THE FIRST DAY OF SCHOOL

O Lord, here I am,
watching my grandchild go to school for the first time today.
I hold tight to his hand, unwilling to let go
yet knowing it's his time to grow.
Help him to get along with his classmates and his teacher.
Open his mind and heart as he learns and plays.
As difficult as it is for me, he's ready
May his guardian angel watch over him and protect him.
Amen.

Bless My Grandchild

AS WE READ TOGETHER

Lord, help my grandchild learn to love
the written word as I read aloud to her.
Let her imagination soar, and
let her find pleasure even in the simple stories.
As I read, I can see her pick up on new words, and
I can see her face light up with excitement.
Learning to read is such an important milestone in her growth.
Help us to embrace this time together as she opens to new
adventures.
Help her find joy in reading.
Amen.

Prayers for Elementary and Middle School Years

To Reach Full Potential

> Our greatest power is our ability to make a
> difference in the lives of the people who pass
> through our lives. Don't let what you *can't* do
> interfere with what you *can* do. Be the differ-
> ence that makes a difference.
>
> —Matthew Kelly

Come Holy Spirit, enlighten my grandchild,
that he may discover his full potential.
Give him the wisdom and the fortitude
to find and use his unique talents.
As he pursues the will of God,
help him to use his gifts to make a difference in the lives of
    others.
O Holy Spirit, each day fill him
with your light and your grace
so that he may become who God made him to be.
Amen.

To Make Good Daily Choices

Therefore, since we are surrounded by so
great a cloud of witnesses, let us rid ourselves of every burden and sin that clings to
us and persevere in running the race that lies
before us while keeping our eyes fixed on
Jesus, the leader and perfecter of faith.
—Hebrews 12:1–2

Dear Lord, young people have so many choices today and
make so many decisions.
Watch over my grandchild's daily choices,
from what she puts on her body
to what she puts in her mind
to what she holds in her heart.
Guide her parents to limit her choices as needed
so that she does not feel overwhelmed.
She is young and needs their help.
Guide her to choose what is right and
not necessarily what is popular.
I am here, Lord, if she needs me.
May she always feel comfortable asking for guidance.
Lead her, Lord.
Amen.

For Commitment

Your heart must be wholly devoted to the
LORD, our God, observing his statutes and
keeping his commandments, as on this day.
—1 Kings 8:61

Dear Lord, there are so many choices and temptations in the
world.
It is difficult for anyone to commit themselves fully to one thing
at a time.
Watch and guide my grandchild.
Help her as she starts new ventures to dedicate her time and
her talent wisely.
Help her to finish what she starts and to stay within the bounds
of her faith.
Guard her heart.
And with everything, may she first choose
to be wholly devoted to your words
so that she is guided to what is right in this life,
to bring her to eternal life with you.
Amen.

For Safety in Playing Sports
(Bl. Pier Giorgio Frassati)

Bl. Pier Giorgio Frassati, intercede to Jesus for my grandchild.
Keep him safe as he plays _____.
Help him to have fun and be fair.
Guide his coach in good sportsmanship.
Whether they win or lose in the field of play,
may he, by your example, learn strength of character.
May he learn that hard work and exercise help him
to prepare to meet life's challenges.
May he learn what it means to work together and
to play together for a common goal.
Amen.

To Use Technology Wisely
(St. Isidore of Seville)

St. Isidore, you helped preserve classical learning by your
    writings.
Intercede for my grandchild as he searches online for answers
and as he interacts with his friends digitally.
Teach him prudence and caution.
Once he pushes the send key, he cannot take back the words.
And some images he may find online are not easily erased or
    forgotten.
May my grandchild be a role model by making good choices.
May he use technology as it is intended,
to gather its preserved wealth of information and
to communicate with friends and family.
Amen.

ST. ISIDORE OF SEVILLE (D. 636)

St. Isidore of Seville was an archbishop and scholar who compiled a twenty-volume encyclopedia. As society was deterio-
rating around him, Isidore wrote about everything in Roman
society and in classical learning to maintain its existence. His
encyclopedia was referred to as the world's first database.

To Cultivate Good Television Habits (St. Clare of Assisi)

St. Clare of Assisi, patron of television,
watch over my grandchild's choices.
Pray for her, that she may use the gift of television
for education and enjoyment and
stay clear of any channels with filth and violence.
May she not confuse what is right and true for what is popular.
Protect her eyes and her ears from anything
that might harm her mind and her heart.
Amen.

ABOUT ST. CLARE OF ASSISI (D. 1253)

Toward the end of her life, Clare of Assisi was too sick to get out of bed. When the sisters left to go to Mass and she was alone, she had a vision. She could see and hear the Mass as it was celebrated just as if she were standing in her stall near the altar in the chapel. Because of this, Pope Pius XII named her the patroness of television.

FOR GOOD FRIENDSHIPS

No one has greater love than this, to lay
down one's life for one's friends. You are my
friends if you do what I command you. I no
longer call you slaves, because a slave does
not know what his master is doing. I have
called you friends, because I have told you
everything I have heard from my Father.
                                        —John 15:13–15

Surrounding ourselves with like-minded friends,
raised with the same values,
is crucial to sustaining our life of faith in you, Lord.
Help my grandson as he finds his way in this world.
Nudge him when he is going down a bad path,
and when he is lonely remind him that he can always rely on
    you,
the One who laid down his life for him.
May my grandson recognize and cultivate friendships
with people who help him become the best he can be.
May he always associate himself with those who love him.
Amen.

AGAINST NEGATIVE PEER PRESSURE

> Am I now currying favor with human beings
> or God? Or am I seeking to please people? If
> I were still trying to please people, I would
> not be a slave of Christ.
>
> —Galatians 1:10

Lord, growing up can be so confusing and challenging.
Right now my grandchild is suffering through a tough time.
His so-called "friends" are tempting him to do what he knows
    isn't right,
just to win their approval.
Help him to make decisions he can be proud of,
choices he can live with.
Help him to make good decisions.
St. Michael the Archangel, defend him in battle!
Amen.

For Courage
(St. George of Lydda)

St. George, you showed great courage defeating the dragon.
Intercede for my grandchild as he faces his fears and anxieties.
Give him the courage to face his most difficult days and
the wisdom and trust to conquer his challenges.
Help him to be strong in his pursuit of all that is true and good.
Amen.

ABOUT ST. GEORGE OF LYDDA (D. 303)

St. George was a great military saint who lived in Palestine in
the fourth century. Legend has it that he made the Sign of the
Cross before slaying a dragon that was terrorizing the town
and threatening to take their princess. Afterward he preached a
powerful sermon that converted thousands of people to Christianity. Legend or not, the point is that evil was overcome by
courage and truth, and beauty reigned.

FOR BALANCE
(ST. JOHN PAUL II)

St. John Paul II, you are the perfect example of balance.
You had an amazing way of enjoying life,
spending time in prayer, reading, and studying.
Watch over my grandchild, and help him to have a strong
    balance
of faith, hard work, and fun.
Help him to have good friends to share fun times
without their influence being destructive in mind, body, or
    spirit.
I pray that he will always stay balanced.
Amen.

ABOUT ST. JOHN PAUL II (D. 2005)

St. John Paul II was pope for twenty-seven years, 1978–2005.
During those years he had many great accomplishments,
including helping to end Communist rule in his homeland,
Poland, and eventually all of Europe. He traveled extensively
during his pontificate, visiting 129 countries, sharing with the
world the importance of spreading the love and peace of Christ.
He was an athlete, an actor, and a writer. He could speak twelve
languages and was as comfortable with a crowd of people as he
was alone in silent prayer.

To Hear Jesus' Call

Come after me, and I will make you fishers
of men.
—Matthew 4:19

Lord, as you called your apostles and they responded by following you,
help my grandchild to have that response.
Daily you call him.
Daily he can choose to hear or not, to respond or not, to follow
or not.
Help my grandchild to hear your voice and to respond to your
call
to follow your will for his life.
Amen.

FOR TRANSITIONS

I command you: be strong and steadfast! Do
not fear nor be dismayed, for the LORD, your
God, is with you wherever you go.

—Joshua 1:9

Lord, help us all to see the good in the changes you allow in
    our lives.
May my grandchild embrace this change and
use it as an opportunity to make new friends and meet new
    people.
May she be open to all you have to offer in her life, and
in return may she offer up any fears and anxieties.
You are all wise, and I see your hand in this transition.
Watch between us. Teach us trust.
Amen.

Prayers for Teenage Years

In High School
(St. Raphael)

St. Raphael the Archangel, you protected Tobiah on his journey.
Protect my grandchild as he navigates high school.
Keep him safe from the many temptations of the world.
Help him in his decision-making
as he attempts to be a role model among his peers.
Help him to stay close to his parents
even though he may feel he doesn't need them as much.
Teens have so many avenues to gain knowledge.
Watch my grandchild so that he may seek truth and hold fast
    to his faith.
Amen.

ABOUT ST. RAPHAEL (ARCHANGEL)

The book of Tobit in the Old Testament reveals St. Raphael as the traveling companion of Tobiah. He frees Tobiah's wife, Sarah, from the devil and heals his father's blindness. The name Raphael means "God heals."

For a First Job Interview

Holy Spirit, guide my grandchild as she goes for her first job
    interview.
It may seem like a small thing, but it's important to her.
I know she is nervous. I know she is excited.
Lead her to make a faith-filled decision,
to serve others in all she does.
Guide her to a place fit to help her learn
responsibility, time management, and respect for authority,
yet where she will also enjoy those with whom she works,
that they may work together for the good of all.
Amen.

FOR GENDER IDENTITY ISSUES

Lord, this world is not for us to fully understand, nor for us to
    control.

You alone see within the heart of my grandchild.

You alone see what's going on inside his mind.

You alone, who created him and love him unconditionally, have
    a plan for his life.

I pray that he will be open to your Holy Spirit.

I pray that he will remain close to you in prayer.

Amen.

WHEN A GRANDCHILD
STARTS DATING

Lord, give my grandchild wisdom as she dates.
Give her wisdom to act as a lady, and
him the courage to act as a gentleman.
Help them to avoid temptations and
to make decisions that keep them from any later regrets.
Let them enjoy responsible, safe fun without drama.
Lord, keep these young people pure in mind, in body, and in
heart.
Amen.

WHEN A GRANDCHILD
STARTS DRIVING
(ST. CHRISTOPHER)

St. Christopher, protect my grandchild
as once you protected the Christ Child,
helping him to reach his destination and return home safely.
Clear him from all distractions,
including his cell phone, music, and friends riding in the car.
Keep him focused on the road,
aware of his surroundings and other drivers.
Help him to drive responsibly,
make smart decisions,
and always—even on the shortest drive—wear his seatbelt.
Amen.

ABOUT ST. CHRISTOPHER (THIRD CENTURY)

St. Christopher was an extremely strong man who, after becoming Christian, lived in a hut next to a raging river and made it his life's work to carry people safely to the other side. According to legend, one day St. Christopher carried the Christ Child safely across the river. He was martyred in the third century, and he is the patron of travelers.

For Choosing a College

Holy Spirit, guide my grandchild to choose a college
that prepares him for his life's work.
Lead him to be happy, to have responsible fun, and to do well.
Guide him as he discerns his vocation and
as he makes a choice that leads him to good experiences.
Help him to choose well.
Amen.

On My Grandchild's Graduation

Lord, my grandchild is graduating high school, and
he and his friends are going their separate ways.
Watch over them as they separate from their parents and from
one another.
They have all done well.
Help them to take the values and faith
handed down by their families and to make good choices.
Help them to find friends with similar values.
Thank you, Lord, for how well my grandchild has done.
I pray that he will continue along a path filled with good, whole-
some habits.
Amen.

For a Grandchild
Leaving Home

Lord, bless my grandchild and her parents
as she prepares to leave home.
Help her parents to let go,
allowing my grandchild to grow,
to spread her wings, and
to become the best person she is capable of being.
Help her to feel secure in her decisions and
to know that she is always welcome home.
Change is often difficult for all involved.
Lord, guide them all to make this as easy as possible.
Amen.

Against Wavering Faith
(St. Monica)

St. Monica, intercede for us and
bring my grandchild back to the Church.
You prayed for your son Augustine, and
he not only returned to the Church,
but he embraced the faith and
turned all those whom he came in contact with to God.
Intercede so that my grandchild may not only believe,
but may live his entire life for Jesus Christ.
Strengthen his love for the scriptures and the teachings of the
Church,
that he may in turn strengthen others.
Amen.

ABOUT ST. MONICA (D. 387)

St. Monica continually fasted and prayed for her husband and her three children. Her husband converted to Christianity on his deathbed, and two of her children entered religious life, while the third, Augustine, strayed far from the Church. However, Monica persisted, following Augustine throughout Italy and asking for help from St. Ambrose. Augustine not only converted but his writings and teachings have made a huge impact in the Church.

FOR AN UNWED PREGNANCY

O dear Lord, my granddaughter has just found out
she's pregnant, and she's not ready for marriage.
A million things are going through her mind.
I know she is frightened.
Give her parents compassion and wisdom.
Guide her, Lord, as she decides how to respond to this news,
whether to raise the baby or look into the option of adoption.
Give the father and his family courage to face this responsibility
    as well, for the good of the child.
I love my grandchild and will support her decision.
Help her decision to be made in love for her unborn child.
Amen.

For a Serious Illness

For nothing will be impossible for God.
—Luke 1:37

Lord, you know the needs of my grandchild.
This situation seems so desperate.
I know you give us your saints to intercede for us.
Surround us with your saints and angels,
to provide comfort and healing.
Whatever is your will, I accept.
But Lord, I'm asking for a miracle.
Amen.

If you wish to pray the St. Rita Novena, turn to page 170, under Traditional Prayers and Novenas.

For a Return to the Faith
(St. Anthony of Padua)

St. Anthony, patron of the lost,
intercede for my grandchild who has lost her way in faith.
Ask the Holy Spirit to lift her up as she wanders aimlessly in
    her beliefs,
filling her anew with wisdom and understanding.
As she struggles to find her place in the Church and to embrace
    her teachings,
open her heart so that she may return to truth.
May the teachings of her childhood and the examples of her
    family
help her to overcome her doubts.
Give us patience to wait with loving hearts.
Good St. Anthony, open her heart and lead my lost grandchild
    back to Christ.
Amen.

ABOUT ST. ANTHONY OF PADUA (D. 1231)

Born to a wealthy family in twelfth-century Portugal, St. Anthony of Padua studied under the Augustinians before becoming a
Franciscan friar. He was a gifted preacher, and he traveled and
taught all over the world to bring many lost souls back to the
Catholic Church. There are miraculous stories of fish gathering
to hear him preach when no one else would listen and a don-
key kneeling as Anthony processed through a town with the
monstrance. Those who witnessed the miracles and listened to

his sermons changed their hearts and returned to the faith. He shows that nothing is impossible with God.

WHEN A FAMILY FACES DIVORCE

Lord, watch over my grandchild
as her parents go through this divorce.
She has been in the midst of the constant arguments,
struggling to stay out of the way,
yet wondering if she should help.
Help her to focus on the love she has for each of them.
There is nothing easy about the separation or the divorce of
    people we love.
Of course, Lord, we pray for possible reconciliation,
to maintain the sanctity of the sacrament.
But if a change of hearts is impossible,
I pray that her parents, my daughter and son-in-law, will find
    a way
to be kind to each other,
to respect each other, and,
mostly, to spend quality time with my grandchild.
Amen.

WHEN THERE IS A DEATH IN THE FAMILY

We do not want you to be unaware, brothers,
about those who have fallen asleep, so that
you may not grieve like the rest, who have
no hope. For if we believe that Jesus died and
rose, so too will God, through Jesus, bring
with him those who have fallen asleep.
—1 Thessalonians 4:13–14

Lord, our family is in such pain right now as we grieve the loss
of _____.
As Christians we believe that death is not the end;
it is the beginning of eternal life with you.
Still, the reality and finality of death is so very painful.
Help us to be gentle with one another and
to give one another the space and time we need.
Help me to comfort my grandchild the way she needs me to.
May her faith in your dying and your rising console her.
And may she know the support of her family during this time
of sadness.
Amen.

Prayers for Adult Grandchildren

Prayer for a Vocation
(St. Alphonsus Liguori)

St. Alphonsus, you changed your vocation several times
over the course of your life,
from being a lawyer,
to founding a congregation,
to preaching and teaching to give people a better understanding
of the love of Jesus and Mary and the saints.
Guide my grandchild to know the will of God for his life.
Whether his vocation is to be a religious, a lawyer, a teacher,
a salesperson, or a stay-at-home dad,
may he know that by serving others well, he serves God.
Guide him to work well with others and
to be a good example of God's love in all he does.
Help him as he discerns his vocation.
Amen.

ABOUT ST. ALPHONSUS LIGUORI (D. 1787)

St. Alphonsus had problems with his sight and chronic asthma
at a young age, which kept him from joining the military. His
father invested in his education, and Alphonsus became a bril-
liant lawyer. He was also a gifted musician and composer. He
decided to leave this all and become a priest and was ordained
at the age of thirty.

In Thanksgiving for the Single Life

Lord, my grandchild has chosen to live the single life.
He has a great job and wonderful friends and
is very content and sure in his choices.
I pray that he will stay close to you, Lord.
I pray that he will live life to the fullest.
I pray that he will always be happy and healthy and fulfilled.
Lord, watch over my grandchild.
Amen.

A Marriage Blessing

Lord, bless these two as they join together in marriage.
I am so happy for my grandchild and her husband.
I pray that they will learn to build each other up and
live a life of joy and happiness.
May their love strengthen each day, and
may they grow together in faith.
May their sorrows be few and their blessings be many.
May they be open to the gift of children, and
may their family be an example of love and service.
Today and every day may they share a life
steeped in faith and family and community.
Amen.

Bless My Grandchild

WHEN A GRANDDAUGHTER BECOMES A MOTHER

> She rises while it is still night, and distributes food to her household, a portion to her maidservants. She picks out a field and acquires it; from her earnings she plants a vineyard. She girds herself with strength; she exerts her arms with vigor.
>
> —Proverbs 31:15–17

Mary, bless my granddaughter as she becomes a mother for the first time.

Help her as she cares for her family.

Oftentimes she will have to put her needs aside for the needs of her child.

Give her the grace to persevere in love and

the strength to give when it is hardest to give.

Mary, your example to give up your life for Christ is our perfect example.

Teach my grandchild to give her all for her child.

Amen.

WHEN A GRANDSON
BECOMES A FATHER

Fathers, do not provoke your children to
anger, but bring them up with the training
and instruction of the Lord.
—Ephesians 6:4

St. Joseph, patron of families, help my grandson as he becomes
  a new father.
Help him to understand the importance
not only of providing for his family monetarily
but also of being there physically
to be a good example of a loving father and husband.
Give him the grace to pass on the faith to his family.
The world needs men with strong convictions
to help build up the family of God.
St. Joseph, teach my grandchild to be a good father.
Amen.

Prayer before an Adult Grandchild's Visit

Dear Lord, my grandchild is coming to visit.
Thank you for this child. Help me to simply love her.
I want to give her advice that I think could help,
but I need to hold my tongue unless asked.
Help me to be a good example
by showing what a Christian home should be and
to just enjoy the visit.
Lord, you made us a family.
Help us to grow in faith together, in hope together, and in love
together.
Amen.

Prayer after an Adult Grandchild's Visit

Dear Lord, my body is exhausted but my heart is full.
Thank you for the time I had with my grandchild.
It's never enough. Bless her and her family as they leave.
May their trip be safe, and
until we meet again, hold them safely in your hands.
Bless this family while we're apart.
Guide them in your ways, and guard them with your love.
Amen.

Prayers for
Serious Needs

For Acceptance
of Imperfections

Jesus answered, "Neither he nor his parents
sinned; it is so that the works of God might
be made visible through him."

—John 9:3

Lord, watch over my grandchild as he struggles.
Ignorance is so often cruel.
Give those around him, who do not understand why he
    struggles,
wisdom and compassion.
Help my grandchild to be surrounded by friends with kind
    hearts.
Help him to strive to use all the gifts you have given,
to excel where he can, and
to manage his frustration for the things he cannot do.
Give him and those around him patience and understanding.
Amen.

Bless My Grandchild

For Parents Fallen
Away from the Faith

Lord, this is difficult.
My grandchild is not being taken to church.
Religion is not a topic that can be discussed.
Lord, help me to step lightly and
to help my grandchild to understand your great love for us and
our need for giving thanks to you.
Help me to subtly share our faith.
Maybe my grandchild can be the example
his parents need to renew their faith.
Show us the way that leads back to you.
Amen.

For a Struggling Marriage (St. Rita of Cascia)

St. Rita, you led a life filled with impossible situations.
My grandchild might feel as if her marriage situation is
impossible.
Fill her with hope. Help her to learn to pray about everything.
Guide her to pray for her marriage and for her husband and
their relationship,
especially when it seems tough.
Help them to remember the love that brought them together.
And if the situation cannot be fixed,
give them the wisdom to be guided by the Church for a solution.
St. Rita, pray for my grandchild.
Amen.

ABOUT ST. RITA OF CASCIA (D. 1457)

St. Rita wanted to join the convent, but in obedience to her
parents she married at age twelve. She was a model wife and
mother despite her abusive husband. After her husband was
murdered and her sons died, she joined a monastery. She bore
the wound of Christ on her forehead.

For a Single Parent
(St. Margaret of Cortona)

St. Margaret of Cortona, you know what it takes to raise a child
  alone.
Watch over my grandchild as she handles being a single parent.
Motherhood is tough enough.
Help me to support without judgment,
to be available when I can, and
to love her unconditionally.
St. Margaret, you handled your struggles
by completely turning to God for help.
Pray for my grandchild to turn to God for all her needs.
Amen.

ABOUT ST. MARGARET OF CORTONA (D. 1297)

When St. Margaret was seven, her mother died. Her father remarried, but she and her stepmother did not like each other. Margaret left home and lived with a man for ten years and had a son with him. When the man was murdered, leaving Margaret to raise her son alone, she changed. She turned to a life of prayer and repentance. Margaret joined the Third Order Franciscans in Cortona, living the rest of her life in poverty, and her son became a friar.

ON THE LOSS OF A PET
(ST. FRANCIS OF ASSISI)

But now ask the beasts to teach you, the birds
of the air to tell you; Or speak to the earth to
instruct you, and the fish of the sea to inform
you. Which of all these does not know that
the hand of God has done this? In his hand
is the soul of every living thing, and the life
breath of all mortal flesh.

—Job 12:7–10

St. Francis of Assisi, you loved all living creatures.
Intercede in love for my grandchild during this difficult time.
Comfort her as she grieves the loss of _____.
She is so sad. My heart aches for her.
Calm her anxieties, and fill her with peace.
Amen.

ABOUT ST. FRANCIS OF ASSISI (D. 1226)

St. Francis truly embodied these verses from Job. He spoke to
the creatures of the earth, loved them, and listened to them. This
is why we pray to him for the needs of our pets or our needs
concerning our pets.

FOR THOSE WITH
EATING DISORDERS

Those live whom the LORD protects; yours
is the life of my spirit. You have given me
health and restored my life!

—Isaiah 38:16

Lord, watch over my grandchild as she struggles with her
 health.
Heal her of this terrible disease.
Protect her from being concerned with what the world says
 she should be,
how the world says she should look.
Help her to love herself, as she is,
in the image of God, your beautiful creation.
These words I repeat for my grandchild,
"Give her health and restore her life!"
I pray that she will feel my love and support during this difficult
 time.
Heal her, Lord.
Amen.

For Those with Cancer (St. Peregrine of Laziosi)

Father, if you are willing, take this cup away
from me; still, not my will but yours be done.
—Luke 22:42

St. Peregrine, patron of those who suffer from cancer,
I beg you to intercede for my grandchild for complete healing.
Her suffering is too much for me to bear.
Help me to be strong for her. Help her parents to be strong.
I have so many questions, so many desires for her in this life.
Ask our merciful God to heal her.
Ask him to heal her suffering, to take this cup away from her.
And help us to feel your presence with us no matter what
    happens.
Amen.

ABOUT ST. PEREGRINE OF LAZIOSI (D. 1345)

St. Peregrine once opposed the papacy, but after receiving forgiveness from St. Philip Benizi, a papal delegate he had injured, he changed his life and his beliefs. After being ordained a priest, he discovered a growth on his right foot, which appeared to be cancerous. The night before the surgery to remove the growth, he spent hours in prayer. As he dozed off, he had a dream that Jesus reached down from the crucifix and touched his foot and healed him. When he awoke, he was healed.

BEFORE AN OPERATION
(STS. COSMAS AND DAMIAN)

Lord, I watch as they roll my grandchild down the hall for her
   operation.
I watch and I pray.
Sts. Cosmas and Damian, intercede for her doctors and nurses.
Guide their skillful hands and their nurturing hearts.
Bring my grandchild through this procedure successfully,
that she may be relieved of all pain.
Heal her completely.
Amen.

ABOUT STS. COSMAS AND DAMIAN
(THIRD CENTURY)

Not much is known about these physicians, who were twin
brothers of Arabian descent and practiced medicine in a Roman
province of Syria. They cured many of the people who came to
them and did not charge for their services. They were martyred
during the rule of Diocletian.

For Those with
Anxiety and Depression
(St. Dymphna)

Lord, there is too much stress put on our children today.
Pressures at school,
nonstop social media and other noise, and
never-ending activity make it hard to find silence.
All of these things only add to children's anxieties and fears
of what it takes to do well, to look good, to fit in, to excel.
St. Dymphna, pray for my grandchild,
who seems to sink right into the frustration and sadness that
      surrounds her.
Pray for her, that God will heal her
of thoughts of hopelessness, anxiety, sadness, anger, and
      frustration.
Help her to see that she is amazing just as she is,
made in the image of God.
Lord, help me to build her confidence, to be a positive influence,
to give her someone to believe in, and to make sure she knows
      that I believe in her.
Who knows the kind of stress she has in her mind and her
      heart?
Cure my grandchild, Lord.
Amen.

ABOUT ST. DYMPHNA (SEVENTH CENTURY)

The daughter of a pagan Irish king and his Christian wife, St. Dymphna consecrated herself to God at the age of fourteen. Shortly after this, her mother died. Her father became mentally ill and wished to marry his daughter, Dymphna. Dymphna fled to safety in the town of Geel in Belgium along with her confessor and two trusted servants. When her father found her and tried to force her to return, she refused—and he killed her along with her companions. In 1349 a church was built in Geel honoring Dymphna, and for more than six hundred years the town has been known for treating and providing help to the mentally ill. She is the patron of those with mental illness, including depression.

On the Death of
a Grandchild's Friend,
with Faith

Lord, my grandchild's friend has died.
She is struggling to understand how this could happen
to someone her age, so young.
May her faith, her belief in you and in heaven, help to comfort
    her.
May time heal all those affected by this sad news.
Lord, deep down, she believes in your mercy and your goodness.
Help her to cling to her faith and
to be a good example of peace and love to her friends.
Heal her sorrowful heart, Lord.
Amen.

On the Death of a Grandchild's Friend, without Faith

Lord, my grandchild's friend has died, and she's angry.
She is struggling to understand how this could happen
to someone her age, so young.
I fear this will drive her further from her own faith.
My grandchild does not want to hear from me
about your mercy or trust or faith.
She's closed us out. All I can do is pray.
Lord Jesus, heal her grief.
Be very close to her as she goes through the process of grieving.
Death is difficult enough, but the death of our young can be
crushing.
Lord, heal her, guard her, and give her wisdom and strength to
push through,
never forgetting her friend but not letting this loss rule her life.
Lord, hold her in your mercy.
Amen.

ON THE DEATH OF MY GREAT-GRANDCHILD

Mary, I am helpless except for prayer.

I understand that my grandchild is angry and confused.

She has carried this child and loved him.

She seems inconsolable since his death.

Heal her mind and her heart at this time of incredibly deep sorrow.

As much as she wants to be left alone,

give her the strength to accept the help and the love of others who just want to "do something."

Mary, you know how she feels,

because you have experienced the loss of a child and know the heartache.

Comfort her, holding her in your mantle,

allowing her to pour out her heart to your heart.

Heal her.

Amen.

Traditional Prayers and Novenas

Introduction

Catholic devotional and prayer practices frequently include the memorized prayers of the saints and other spiritual writers. These prayers are passed from one generation to the next as part of our spiritual legacy. While many of us can and do speak to God directly from the heart, in our own words, there can be something comforting and secure about invoking the tried-and-true words of those who have gone before us.

Similarly, the origins of a form of prayer known as a *novena* (for "nine," the standard number of days a particular prayer is offered) can be traced to the earliest days of Christianity. Novenas are frequently associated with a particular patron saint.

This final section of the book includes some of the most common prayers and novenas that you, as a grandparent, may wish to use as you continue to pray for your grandchild and his family as well as for your own intentions. May they bring you a measure of reassurance, comfort, and grace in your time of need, knowing that you are praying in communion with others all over the world.

Prayers

ACT OF CONSECRATION TO OUR LADY OF THE MIRACULOUS MEDAL

As a sign of their devotion to the Blessed Mother, some choose to consecrate themselves and their spiritual gifts to Mary, often on November 27 (the Feast of Our Lady of the Miraculous Medal) or on one of her feast days throughout the year.

O Virgin Mother of God, Mary Immaculate, we dedicate and consecrate
ourselves to you under the title of Our Lady of the Miraculous Medal.
May this Medal be for each one of us a sure sign of your affection for us and
a constant reminder of our duties toward you.
Ever while wearing it, may we be blessed
by your loving protection and preserved in the grace of your Son.
O Savior, keep us close to you every moment of our lives.
Obtain for us, your children, the grace of a happy death
so that, in union with you, we may enjoy the bliss of heaven forever.
Amen.
O Mary, conceived without sin,
pray for us who have recourse to you. *(Repeat 3 times.)*

ACT OF CONSECRATION
TO THE SACRED HEART OF JESUS

As the side of Jesus opened on the Cross to reveal his Sacred Heart, may our families in return open our hearts to him. May our families speak to his most Sacred Heart. May we love him heart to heart, and may our families be a reflection of his most Sacred Heart and spread his love to all. We need to consecrate our families to the Sacred Heart, and every home should display an image of the Sacred Heart of Jesus.

I give myself and consecrate to the Sacred Heart of our Lord
    Jesus Christ,
my person and my life, my actions, pains, and sufferings,
so that I may be unwilling to make use of any part of my being
other than to honor, love, and glorify the Sacred Heart.
This is my unchanging purpose—namely, to be all his, and
to do all things for the love of him,
at the same time renouncing with all my heart whatever is dis-
    pleasing to him.
I therefore take you, O Sacred Heart, to be the only object of
    my love,
the guardian of my life, my assurance of salvation,
the remedy of my weakness and inconstancy,
the atonement for all the faults of my life, and
my sure refuge at the hour of death.
Be then, O Heart of goodness, my justification before God the
    Father, and

turn away from me the strokes of his righteous anger.
O Heart of love, I put my confidence in you,
for I fear everything from my own wickedness and frailty,
but I hope for all things from your goodness and bounty.
Remove from me all that can displease you or resist your holy
    will;
let your pure love imprint your image so deeply upon my heart
that I may never be able to forget you or be separated from you.
May I obtain from all your loving kindness
the grace of having my name written in your heart,
for in you I desire to place all my happiness and glory,
living and dying in bondage to you.
Amen.

For more information about the Sacred Heart devotion or how to make a consecration to the Sacred Heart, see the website of the Sacred Heart Enthronement Network (https://enthronements. com).

THE ANGELUS

Like other traditional prayers at set hours of the day, the Angelus unites those who pray it throughout the world. When we stop our busy day at noon to take a moment in prayer to honor Our Lady, we please God. May we pass this tradition on to our grandchildren. (This prayer is offered as a response, with the leader reading the "V" and the rest reading "R," followed by a "Hail Mary" in unison.)

V. The Angel of the Lord declared unto Mary,

R. And she conceived of the Holy Spirit.

Hail Mary . . .

V. Behold the handmaid of the Lord.

R. Be it done unto me according to thy Word.

Hail Mary . . .

V. And the Word was made flesh,

R. And dwelt among us.

Hail Mary . . .

V. Pray for us, O holy Mother of God.

R. That we may be made worthy of the promises of Christ.

V. Let us pray:

All: Pour forth, we beseech you, O Lord, Thy grace into our hearts,

that we, to whom the Incarnation of Christ,

Thy Son, was made known by the message of an angel,

may by his Passion and Cross

be brought to the glory of his Resurrection.

Through the same Christ, our Lord.
Amen.

Anima Christi

Soul of Christ, make me holy.
Body of Christ, be my salvation.
Blood of Christ, let me drink your wine.
Water flowing from the side of Christ, wash me clean.
Passion of Christ, strengthen me.
Kind Jesus, hear my prayer.
Hide me within your wound and keep me close to you.
Defend me from the evil enemy.
Call me at my death to the fellowship of your saints,
that I may sing your praise with them
and through all eternity.
Amen.

This traditional prayer has been adapted for praying for a grandchild on the next page.

Anima Christi
for My Grandchild

Soul of Christ, make holy my grandchild.
Body of Christ, save her.
Blood of Christ, overfill her cup of graces.
Water from the side of Christ, cleanse her.
Passion of Christ, strengthen her.
O Good Jesus, hear her prayer.
Within your wounds hide her.
Permit her not to be separated from you.
From the wicked foe, defend her in the daily battles of life.
At the hour of her death, call her
and bid her come to you,
that with your saints she may praise you
forever and ever.
Amen.

CHAPLET OF DIVINE MERCY

The Chaplet of Divine Mercy was given to St. Faustina Kowalska, as recorded in her Diary *(paragraph 476), first published in 1981. The prayers may be offered on rosary beads, as indicated below, for nine consecutive days (like a novena) if desired.*

1. *Make the Sign of the Cross.*
2. *(Opening Prayer)* "You expired, Jesus, but the source of life gushed forth for souls, and the ocean of mercy opened up for the whole world. O Fount of Life, unfathomable Divine Mercy, envelop the whole world and empty yourself out upon us."
3. *(Then, on each of the first three beads)* "O Blood and Water, which gushed forth from the Heart of Jesus as a fount of mercy for us, I trust in you!"
4. *(On the center medallion)* Say one "Our Father," one "Hail Mary," and the Apostles' Creed.
5. *(On the first large bead)* "Eternal Father, I offer you the Body and Blood, Soul and Divinity, of your dearly beloved Son, Our Lord, Jesus Christ, in atonement for our sins and those of the whole world."
6. *(On the ten small beads)* "For the sake of his sorrowful Passion, have mercy on us and on the whole world."
7. *Repeat steps 5–6 for the remaining four decades.*
8. *(Concluding Prayer—repeat three times)* "Holy God, Holy Mighty One, Holy Immortal One, have mercy on us and on the whole world."

9. *(Optional Closing Prayer)* "Eternal God, in whom mercy is endless and the treasury of compassion inexhaustible, look kindly upon us and increase your mercy in us, that in difficult moments we might not despair nor become despondent, but with great confidence submit ourselves to your holy will, which is Love and Mercy itself."

Guardian Angel Prayer

This is a beautiful prayer to teach your grandchildren.

Angel of God, my guardian dear,
to whom his love commits me here,
ever this day (or night) be at my side,
to light and guard, to rule and guide.
Amen.

Consecration of the Family

Consecrating ourselves and our families to Jesus and Mary and Joseph can only strengthen the family bond. When we are strong, we can be strong for others. (Lord, may these Acts of Consecration give our families, especially our children and grandchildren, the grace they need to dedicate themselves to you in this life so as to gain eternal life with you in the next.)

O Jesus, our most loving Redeemer,
you came to enlighten the world with your teaching and
    example.
You willed to spend the greater part of your life in humble
    obedience
to Mary and Joseph in the poor home of Nazareth.
In this way you sanctified the family,
which was to be an example for all Christian families.
Jesus, Mary, Joseph! Graciously accept our family,
which we dedicate and consecrate to you.
Be pleased to protect, guard, and keep it
in sincere faith, in peace, and in the harmony of Christian
    charity.
By conforming ourselves to the divine model of your family,
may we all attain to eternal happiness.
Mary, Mother of Jesus and our mother,
by your merciful intercession make this our humble offering
acceptable to Jesus, and obtain for us graces and blessings.
St. Joseph, most holy guardian of Jesus and Mary,
help us by your prayers in all our spiritual and temporal needs

so that we may praise Jesus, our divine Savior,
together with Mary and you for all eternity.
Amen.

MARY, UNDOER OF KNOTS

Holy Mary, full of God's presence during the days of your life,
you accepted with full humility the Father's will, and
the devil was never capable to tie you around with his confusion.
Once with your Son you interceded for our difficulties, and,
full of kindness and patience, you gave us examples
of how to untie the knots of our life.
And by remaining forever our mother,
you put in order and make clear the ties that link us to the Lord.
Holy Mary, Mother of God, and our mother,
you who untie with a motherly heart the knots of our life,
we pray to you to receive in your hands *(name your grandchild)*,
and to free him/her of the knots and confusion with which our
enemy attacks.
Through your grace, your intercession, and your example,
deliver us from all evil, Our Lady, and untie the knots
that prevent us from being united with God
so that we, free from sin and error, may find him in all things,
may have our hearts placed in him, and
may serve him always in our brothers and sisters.
Amen.

Padre Pio Prayer
for My Grandchild

O God, you gave St. Pio of Pietrelcina, Capuchin priest,
the great privilege of participating in a unique way
in the Passion of your Son.
Grant my grandchild through his intercession
the grace of *(state your desire for your grandchild)*,
which she ardently desires; and
above all grant her the grace of living in conformity
with the death of Jesus, to arrive at the glory of the resurrection.
Pray 3 Glory Bes

ABOUT PADRE PIO OF PIETRELCINA (D. 1968)

St. Padre Pio was an Italian Capuchin who bore the wounds of
Christ, the stigmata, on his hands, feet, and side. As a spiritual
director, he led others to desire the will of God and to see God
in all things. He had five simple rules for spiritual growth: weekly confession, daily Communion, spiritual reading, meditation,
and examination of conscience (preferably twice a day, morning
and evening). May he be our example!

Rosary for My Grandchild

In joy and in sorrow, the Rosary is Our Lady's gift to her children—and it is a powerful weapon in the hands of a praying grandmother! I assume you already know the basic prayers of the Rosary (Apostles' Creed, Our Father, Glory Be, Hail Mary, and the Fatima Prayer that begins, "O my Jesus . . ."). Therefore, I list here only the brief meditations associated with each of the mysteries, to be read as you begin each decade.

JOYFUL MYSTERIES

(For meditation on Mondays and Saturdays)

1. The Annunciation

Mary said, "Behold, I am the handmaid of
the Lord. May it be done to me according to
your word."

—Luke 1:38

Mary, help my grandchild to know the will of God in his life and to follow his call. Teach him to listen with his heart, especially when he does not fully understand where the Holy Spirit is leading him. Like you, may he hear the voice of his guardian calming his fears.

1 Our Father, 10 Hail Marys, 1 Glory Be

2. The Visitation

When Elizabeth heard Mary's greeting, the
infant leaped in her womb, and Elizabeth,
filled with the Holy Spirit, cried out in a
loud voice and said, "Most blessed are you
among women, and blessed is the fruit of
your womb. And how does this happen to
me, that the mother of my Lord should come
to me?"

—Luke 1:41–43

Mary, you showed great charity visiting your cousin and staying
with her for three months while she was pregnant. Visits teach
us to put others first. May my grandchild be encouraged to offer
up her time for others.
1 Our Father, 10 Hail Marys, 1 Glory Be

3. The Birth of Jesus

While they were there, the time came for her
to have her child, and she gave birth to her
firstborn son. She wrapped him in swaddling
clothes and laid him in a manger, because
there was no room for them in the inn.

—Luke 2:6–7

Mary, you show us that no matter how poor we are in our spiritual life, Jesus wants to dwell in us. May my grandchild always

make room for Jesus. May he allow Jesus to enter his daily life, to save him from his poverty of spirit.
1 Our Father, 10 Hail Marys, 1 Glory Be

4. The Presentation in the Temple

When the days were completed for their
purification according to the law of Moses,
they took him up to Jerusalem to present
him to the Lord.

—Luke 2:22

Mary, I present my grandchild to the Father just as you presented your Son, Jesus. May she follow the scriptures, have faith in the commandments, and love the faith. May she be holy and draw others to your Son.
1 Our Father, 10 Hail Marys, 1 Glory Be

5. The Finding of the Child Jesus in the Temple

After three days they found him in the
temple, sitting in the midst of the teachers,
listening to them and asking them questions,
and all who heard him were astounded at his
understanding and his answers.

—Luke 2:46–47

Mary, help my grandchild to always seek Jesus. When he is lost, give him the wisdom to understand that all he needs can be

found in God's presence. When he is filled with hopelessness and is hungering for something more in his life, may he simply go to your Son.
1 Our Father, 10 Hail Marys, 1 Glory Be

SORROWFUL MYSTERIES

(For meditation on Tuesdays and Fridays)

1. Agony in the Garden

He advanced a little and fell prostrate in prayer, saying, "My Father, if it is possible, let this cup pass from me; yet, not as I will, but as you will."

—Matthew 26:39

Mary, strengthen my grandchild so that she may be open to the will of God. As she prays for understanding, give her a glimpse of peace, something to cling to, a hint that she is going in the right direction. Give her hope in prayer.
1 Our Father, 10 Hail Marys, 1 Glory Be

2. Scourging at the Pillar

But he was pierced for our sins, crushed for our iniquity. He bore the punishment that

makes us whole, by his wounds
we were healed.

—Isaiah 53:5

Mary, your son sacrificed himself for us because he loves us.
I cannot imagine what it was like for you, seeing your son
stripped and beaten. Help my grandchild to understand the
saving power of such love. Instill in him a heart that is pure
and loving and kind. Help him to return again and again to be
reconciled and to be healed.

1 Our Father, 10 Hail Marys, 1 Glory Be

3. Crowning with Thorns

And the soldiers wove a crown out of thorns
and placed it on his head, and clothed him
in a purple cloak, and they came to him
and said, "Hail, King of the Jews!" And they
struck him repeatedly.

—John 19:2–3

Mary, your son endured the pain from the sharp thorns and
the repeated beating. If it is possible, pray that my grandchild
may be spared such terrible pain and ridicule. Keep her safe
from those who can hurt her physically, mentally, or spiritually.

1 Our Father, 10 Hail Marys, 1 Glory Be

4. Carrying of the Cross

And when they had mocked him, they
stripped him of the cloak, dressed him in his
own clothes, and led him off to crucify him.
As they were going out, they met a Cyrenian
named Simon; this man they pressed into
service to carry his cross.
—Matthew 27:31–32

Mary, there are so many people we meet every day who are
carrying crosses, handling burdens. Help my grandchild to be
like Simon, to reach out to be of service and make a difference.
1 Our Father, 10 Hail Marys, 1 Glory Be

5. Crucifixion

So they took Jesus, and carrying the cross
himself he went out to what is called the
Place of the Skull, in Hebrew, Golgotha.
There they crucified him, and with him two
others, one on either side, with Jesus
in the middle.
—John 19:16–18

Mary, I cannot imagine your sorrow, seeing your son crucified.
Each time my grandchild looks at the cross, may she remember
all your Son has done for us. May it be for her a challenge to be

unselfish and to love unconditionally for the sake of the One who gave his life for us.

1 Our Father, 10 Hail Marys, 1 Glory Be

GLORIOUS MYSTERIES

(For meditation on Wednesdays and Sundays)

1. The Resurrection

Then the angel said to the women in reply,
"Do not be afraid! I know that you are seeking Jesus the crucified. He is not here, for he
has been raised just as he said. Come and see
the place where he lay."

—Matthew 28:5–6

Mary, help my grandchild not to be afraid to share his faith with his friends and his family and his community. We need good witnesses to the resurrected Christ. We need young people with strong faith, more who come and see and tell others.

1 Our Father, 10 Hail Marys, 1 Glory Be

2. The Ascension

As he blessed them he parted from them and
was taken up to heaven.

—Luke 24:51

Mary, as your son ascended to prepare a place for us in eternity, he gave hope to our broken world. Help my grandchild to strive for holiness. Increase in her the virtue of hope. Help her to believe that we are working for something better here. Raise her up.

1 Our Father, 10 Hail Marys, 1 Glory Be

3. The Descent of the Holy Spirit

The Advocate, the Holy Spirit that the Father
will send in my name—he will teach you
everything and remind you of all that [I]
told you.

—John 14:26

Mary, your Son sent his Spirit for us. Open my grandchild's heart to receive and to believe all that the Spirit teaches, and by the Spirit to persevere in using the gifts we received at baptism.

1 Our Father, 10 Hail Marys, 1 Glory Be

4. The Assumption

A great sign appeared in the sky, a woman
clothed with the sun, with the moon under
her feet, and on her head a crown of
twelve stars.

—Revelation 12:1

Mary, you are a sign from heaven, seated in glory, ready to intercede for us. As our mother, you want all that is good for us. Help my grandchild as she prays for the needs in her life. You know what is good for her. Help her to trust that you will take her prayers to God and that she will be nourished and comforted and loved.

1 Our Father, 10 Hail Marys, 1 Glory Be

5. *The Crowning of the Blessed Virgin Mary*

I will rejoice heartily in the LORD, my being
exults in my God; For he has clothed me
with garments of salvation, and wrapped
me in a robe of justice, Like a bridegroom
adorned with a diadem, as a bride adorns
herself with her jewels.

—Isaiah 61:10

Mary, Queen of Heaven, you are the perfect example of holiness. You are our protection, our Queen Mother. You advocated for us to bring us to holiness, to help us gain heaven. Nourish my grandchild in your tender mercy. Hold him in your mantle and keep him safe from all harm. Protect his heart and guide him to holiness.

1 Our Father, 10 Hail Marys, 1 Glory Be

LUMINOUS MYSTERIES

(For meditation on Thursdays)

1. The Baptism of Christ

John tried to prevent him, saying, "I need to
be baptized by you, and yet you are coming
to me?" Jesus said to him in reply, "Allow it
now, for thus it is fitting for us to fulfill all
righteousness." Then he allowed him. After
Jesus was baptized, he came up from the
water and behold, the heavens were opened
[for him], and he saw the Spirit of God
descending like a dove [and] coming
upon him.

—Matthew 4:14–16

Mary, help my grandchild to keep his baptismal promises and
to renew them through the sacrament of Reconciliation. Guide
him in this life so that one day he too may hear, "This is my
beloved Son, with whom I am well pleased."
1 Our Father, 10 Hail Marys, 1 Glory Be

2. The Miracle at Cana

Jesus and his disciples were also invited to
the wedding. When the wine ran short, the
mother of Jesus said to him, "They have no
wine." [And] Jesus said to her, "Woman, how

does your concern affect me? My hour has
not yet come." His mother said to the servers, "Do whatever he tells you."
—John 2:2–5

Mary, your son fulfilled your request at the marriage feast out
of obedience and respect. Teach my grandchild to have the
same obedience and respect. Help her to listen and to hear and
to act. Just as Jesus changed the water into the best wine of the
celebration, I ask that you fill my grandchild with all she needs
to be her best.
1 Our Father, 10 Hail Marys, 1 Glory Be

3. The Proclamation of the Kingdom of God

This is the time of fulfillment. The kingdom
of God is at hand. Repent, and believe
in the gospel.
—Mark 1:15

Mary, we are called to continue the ministry of proclaiming the
Good News of God's kingdom. Help my grandchild to witness
to Christ. Help him to believe in the power of the Spirit and to
continue the work of Jesus.
1 Our Father, 10 Hail Marys, 1 Glory Be

4. The Transfiguration

After six days Jesus took Peter, James, and
John his brother, and led them up a high
mountain by themselves. And he was transfigured before them; his face shone like the
sun and his clothes became white as light.
—Matthew 17:1–2

Mary, your son is transfigured before us, revealing himself to
us as both human and divine. Bless my grandchild each day.
May she be open to newness, to likeness in Christ, to change
for the better. Help her to start each day refreshed in the Spirit,
seeking purity as she encounters Jesus Christ through prayer
and through relationships with others.
1 Our Father, 10 Hail Marys, 1 Glory Be

5. The Institution of the Eucharist

When the hour came, he took his place at
table with the apostles. He said to them, "I
have eagerly desired to eat this Passover with
you before I suffer, for, I tell you, I shall not
eat it [again] until there is fulfillment in the
kingdom of God." Then he took a cup, gave
thanks, and said, "Take this and share it
among yourselves."
—Luke 22:14–17

Mary, pray that my grandchild will always have a love for the Eucharist. Let his participation in the Mass be a joy for your son. I pray that he will be a Christlike witness to his friends and family. Your son thirsts for us to be close to him. How much closer can we be than at his table, receiving him?

1 Our Father, 10 Hail Marys, 1 Glory Be

St. Michael Prayer
(Against Evil)

Yours is the gigantic task of overcoming all
evil with good, always trying amidst the
problems of life to place your trust in God,
knowing that his grace supplies strength to
human weakness. You must oppose every
form of hatred with the invincible power of
Christ's love.

—St. John Paul II

St. Michael the Archangel,
defend us in battle;
be our defense against the wickedness and snares of the devil.
May God rebuke him, we humbly pray,
and do thou, O Prince of the heavenly host,
by the power of God, thrust into hell Satan,
and the other evil spirits, who prowl about the world
seeking the ruin of souls.
Amen.

ABOUT ST. MICHAEL

St. Michael is the leader of all the angels. He is seen in the
Old Testament Book of Daniel as the helper and protector of
the Chosen people. He appears in the New Testament fighting
against evil. Throughout history, the Church has prayed to St.
Michael the Archangel for protection against evil.

Bless My Grandchild

St. Patrick's Breastplate

I bind unto myself today the power of God to hold and lead,
his eye to watch, his might to stay, his ear to hearken to my
    need,
the wisdom of my God to teach, his hand to guide, his shield
    to ward,
the word of God to give me speech, his heav'nly host to be my
    guard.
Christ be with me, Christ within me,
Christ behind me, Christ before me,
Christ beside me, Christ to win me,
Christ to comfort and restore me.
Christ beneath me, Christ above me,
Christ in hearts of all that love me,
Christ in mouth of friend and stranger.
I bind unto myself the name, the strong name of the Trinity
by invocation of the same, the Three in One and One in Three,
of whom all nature has creation, eternal Father, Spirit, Word.
Praise to the Lord of my salvation; salvation is of Christ the
    Lord.
Amen.

*This traditional prayer has been adapted on the next page for
praying for a grandchild.*

St. Patrick's Breastplate
for My Grandchild

Christ be his protection with each encounter,
with every move and in every occasion.
Christ with him, Christ before him.
Christ behind him, Christ in him.
Christ beneath him, Christ above him.
Christ on his right, Christ on his left.
Christ when he lies down,
Christ when he sits down,
Christ when he arises.
Christ in the heart of every man who thinks of him.
Christ in the mouth of everyone who speaks of him.
Christ in every eye that sees him.
Christ in every ear that hears him.
He arises today through a mighty strength,
the invocation of the Trinity,
through belief in the Threeness,
through confession of the Oneness of the Creator of creation.
Amen.

ABOUT ST. PATRICK

St. Patrick was born in Roman Britain and at the age of sixteen
was kidnapped and taken to Ireland as a slave. After six years,
he escaped, returned to Britain, studied at a monastery and was
ordained into the priesthood. In his forties, he returned to Ireland, working to change the pagan country to Christianity. He

lived in constant danger of martyrdom but continually thanked God for choosing him to be an instrument of his love.

From St. Teresa of Avila's Bookmark (For a Worried Grandchild)

St. Teresa, my grandchild seems stressed and worried.
May she cling to faith in God alone as you did.
Let nothing disturb her; let nothing frighten her.
All things are passing; God alone is changeless.
Patience gains all things.
Who has God wants nothing.
God alone suffices.
Amen.

St. Teresa of Avila Prayer

Christ has no body now on earth but yours,
no hands but yours, no feet but yours.
Yours are the eyes through which the compassion of Christ
must look out on the world.
Yours are the feet with which he is to go about doing good.
Yours are the hands with which he is to bless his people.
Amen.

ABOUT ST. TERESA OF AVILA

Teresa of Avila was one of the first women given the title Doctor of the Church. As a Carmelite nun, she was not satisfied with how lax the order had become. She not only reformed the Carmelite Order but founded sixteen new convents based on her stricter rule. Despite her extensive travels, she was a great writer and maintained a deep contemplative life.

Stations of the Cross for My Grandchild

The Stations of the Cross can be found on the grounds of your local parish. Walking the stations is a beautiful devotional practice, not only during Lent but also on Fridays throughout the year. After each of the reflections below, the group responds with the prayer, "We adore you, O Christ, and we praise you because by your Holy Cross, you have redeemed the world."

FIRST STATION

Jesus Is Condemned to Death

Matthew 27:26, Mark 15:15, Luke 23:23–25, John 19:16

Jesus, you obeyed your Father even though it meant embracing the Cross. May my grandchild have the courage to embrace her faith when others make fun of her or wrongly accuse her. *We adore you . . .*

SECOND STATION

Jesus Is Made to Carry His Cross

John 19:17

Jesus, help us to carry our crosses. Help my grandchild to accept his daily discomforts and challenges with patience and resignation. He will experience setbacks and disappointments in this life. May he look to you on the cross for perseverance and courage.

We adore you . . .

THIRD STATION

Jesus Falls the First Time

Matthew 27:31

Jesus, give us strength. Help my grandchild as she carries her load of school, work, and daily struggles. Help her to accept failure with humility and to come to you for all her needs, no matter how big or small. With your help, may she always pick herself up and move toward the goal of eternal glory.

We adore you . . .

FOURTH STATION

Jesus Meets His Sorrowful Mother

John 19:25–27

Jesus, grant us the grace of a truly devoted love for your mother. It pains me to watch my grandchild suffer, but I know I cannot do everything for him. He has to bear certain pains in life to help him grow. Watching is difficult. Help him through it. Quickly.

We adore you . . .

FIFTH STATION

Simon Helps Jesus to Carry the Cross

Matthew 27:32, Mark 15:21, Luke 23:26

Jesus, we want to be of help to you here and now. Every time my grandchild steps forth to help another person, may he have the strength of Simon. Even if he doesn't want to help, let him not turn away from someone in need. Give him the grace, Jesus, one step at a time.

We adore you . . .

SIXTH STATION

Veronica Wipes the Face of Jesus

Luke 23:27

Jesus, the sight of your bloodied face is difficult to stomach. Help my grandchild to look past the ugly and disfigured. Help her to see through the eyes, into the heart, and to love others no matter what they look like. Teach her to be Veronica, to see with compassion and love, and to have no fear in her actions. *We adore you . . .*

SEVENTH STATION

Jesus Falls the Second Time

Luke 23:26

Lord, bless my grandchild with the courage to persevere in grace. Crosses in life are often difficult to accept. May he accept his with dignity and help others to do the same. May he look beyond himself and help to raise up others in faith and charity. *We adore you . . .*

EIGHTH STATION

Jesus Speaks to the Women of Jerusalem

Luke 23:28–31

Lord, you stopped to show compassion for others during an incredible trial of your own. May my grandchild be aware of those in the crowd. May she show compassion and love to those in need. Give her a strong sense of charity.
We adore you . . .

NINTH STATION

Jesus Falls for the Third Time

John 19:17

Lord, you manage to rise, to find strength in your darkest hour. Help my grandchild to learn from the cross. Teach him that no matter how many times in life he is challenged, no matter how difficult it gets, he can look to you and rise above. Any time he falls, Lord, help him to begin anew.
We adore you . . .

TENTH STATION

Jesus Is Stripped of His Garments

Luke 23:24

Lord, you were stripped of what was left of your possessions, dying and rising in glory to eternal life. May my grandchild be able to separate herself from earthly pleasures that may cause her harm. May she learn to detach from the world and focus on the path to righteousness and justice. May she win the glory you have gained for us.

We adore you . . .

ELEVENTH STATION

Jesus Is Nailed to the Cross

Matthew 27:33–38, Mark 15:22–27, Luke 23:33–34, John 19:18

Lord, you were beaten, stripped, and then pierced by nails to a cross. As we contemplate your suffering, may we gain hearts of compassion for all who suffer in this world. Help my grandchild to understand all you have done for us and to have a grateful heart, repaying you by honoring and obeying your words in holy scripture.

We adore you . . .

TWELFTH STATION

Jesus Dies on the Cross

Matthew 27:46–50, Mark 15:34–37, Luke 23:46, John 19:28–30

Lord, you died for us because you love us. Help my grandchild
to understand that kind of deep love and to love you in return.
Completely. Unconditionally. Help him to love his friends and
his family as well. There is no greater love than to give one's all
for another. Help my grandchild to give life his all.
We adore you . . .

THIRTEENTH STATION

Jesus Is Taken Down from the Cross

Matthew 27:57–58, Mark 15:42–45, Luke 28:50–52, John 19:38

Lord, your mother received you into her arms at the base of the
cross. Help my grandchild to know that I am here for her if she
needs me. I am at the foot of her crosses, praying for her, loving
her, knowing that you will help her through it all.
We adore you . . .

FOURTEENTH STATION

Jesus Is Placed in the Tomb

Matthew 27:59–61, Mark 15:46–47, Luke 23:53–56, John 19:39–42

Lord, as your body is anointed and placed in the tomb, may your burial be an example of the reverence and respect we must have for those who have died. May my grandchild understand the importance of praying for those who have died and of visiting those in mourning. Help him to be considerate of those who experience losses in their lives.

We adore you . . .

FIFTEENTH STATION

The Resurrection

Matthew 28, Mark 16, Luke 24, John 20

Lord, by your rising from the dead, you bring us life. You have conquered death, and now we know there is something more for us after our life on earth. Help my grandchild to grasp the truth of your rising so that she will work on this earth to obtain the gift of heaven. You can help her rise above the sufferings in this life. You can heal her sinfulness. You can bring her to eternal life. You, Lord, are all we need.

We adore you . . .

Novenas

A NINE-DAY NOVENA
FOR A GRANDCHILD'S NEEDS

Novenas are nine consecutive days or nine hours of prayer invoking the intercession of Jesus or Mary or one of the saints. These prayers may be said as written for nine days, or you may choose to focus each day's prayer on the one saint who meets the specific need of your grandchild. Would one of these patrons be a good "fit" for your grandchild?

- St. Monica—for a grandchild to return to the Church
- St. Raphael—for a teenage grandchild's safety
- St. Kateri Tekakwitha—for a grandchild to be strong in faith
- St. Benedict—for a grandchild's closer union with God through good habits
- St. Ignatius of Loyola—for a grandchild to discern the will of God
- St. Maximillian Kolbe—for a grandchild to stay close to Mary and live unselfishly
- St. Martin of Tours—for a grandchild to be generous
- Mary—for a grandchild to be open to the will of God
- St. John Paul II—for a grandchild to practice forgiveness

DAY ONE

St. Monica, you fervently prayed for your son Augustine to return to the Church. Not only did he return, but he became a saint! I pray that my grandchild may return to the Church. I pray that she will find her way back to the love of Christ waiting for her, believing in her, loving her. Intercede for me and obtain from God the desire I have for my grandchild *(mention your specific request here)*.

Pray 3 Our Fathers, 3 Hail Marys, 3 Glory Bes

DAY TWO

St. Raphael, you guarded the teenage boy Tobiah as he traveled to a far-off country. You protected him from evil. Intercede for my grandchild as he navigates this world. Protect him from harm. Intercede for me and obtain from God the desire I have for my grandchild *(mention your specific request here)*.

Pray 3 Our Fathers, 3 Hail Marys, 3 Glory Bes

DAY THREE

St. Kateri Tekakwitha, your conversion was an incredible example to everyone you encountered. Your dedication to Mass and Communion proved your strength of faith. Intercede for my grandchild, that she might love Jesus Christ as you loved him. Strengthen her desire for prayer and for Mass and Communion. Intercede for me and obtain from God the desire I have for my grandchild *(mention your specific request here)*.

Pray 3 Our Fathers, 3 Hail Marys, 3 Glory Bes

DAY FOUR

St. Benedict, you taught a regular routine of prayer, work, study, and rest, which brings us all to closer union with God. Oh, how I would love my grandchild to have this kind of routine or anything close to it! Intercede for my grandchild, that he may discover the joy of a daily spiritual routine. Strengthen his love for Christ and his love for prayer. Intercede for me and obtain from God the desire I have for my grandchild *(mention your specific request here)*.

Pray 3 Our Fathers, 3 Hail Marys, 3 Glory Bes

DAY FIVE

St. Ignatius of Loyola, you wrote the *Spiritual Exercises* to examine your life and draw you closer to God. Intercede for my grandchild, that she may occasionally reexamine her life to discern the will of God. We can all just sail through life believing we're doing the right thing; or, through prayer and sacrifice, we can learn God's will. Intercede for me and obtain from God the desire I have for my grandchild *(mention your specific request here)*.

Pray 3 Our Fathers, 3 Hail Marys, 3 Glory Bes

DAY SIX

St. Maximillian Kolbe, you taught others the importance of a relationship with Mary, the Mother of God. You sacrificed so that others could have life. Intercede for my grandchild, that he may live an unselfish life. May he draw close to Mary and learn to choose what is right. Intercede for me and obtain from God the desire I have for my grandchild *(mention your specific request here).*

Pray 3 Our Fathers, 3 Hail Marys, 3 Glory Bes

DAY SEVEN

St. Martin of Tours, you gave half of your cloak to a poor beggar on the side of the road, in a spontaneous act of kindness. Intercede for my grandchild, that she may naturally be generous, especially to the poor and underserved. Help her to give without expecting anything in return. Intercede for me and obtain from God the desire I have for my grandchild *(mention your specific request here).*

Pray 3 Our Fathers, 3 Hail Marys, 3 Glory Bes

DAY EIGHT

Mary, your yes to the will of God, to offering yourself for another, is our greatest example of trust. Help my grandchild to open his heart to God's will in his life and to trust in you to protect and guide him. Keep him in your care, safe from evil and working toward holiness. Intercede for me and obtain from God the desire I have for my grandchild *(mention your specific request here).*

Pray 3 Our Fathers, 3 Hail Marys, 3 Glory Bes

DAY NINE

St. John Paul II, you humbled yourself as you forgave the man who shot you. Help us to forgive one another. Intercede for my grandchild as she learns to put aside any pettiness and grudges, learning to forgive and forget. True forgiveness is never easy but is necessary to move forward in life and to grow in love. Intercede for me and obtain from God the desire I have for my grandchild *(mention your specific request here).*
Pray 3 Our Fathers, 3 Hail Marys, 3 Glory Bes

NOVENA TO OUR LADY OF LOURDES (FOR HEALING)

O ever-Immaculate Virgin, Mother of Mercy,
health of the sick, refuge of sinners, comforter of the afflicted,
you know our wants, our troubles, our sufferings;
look with mercy on my grandchild.
By appearing in the Grotto of Lourdes,
you were pleased to make it a privileged sanctuary,
whence you dispense your favors; and
already many sufferers have obtained the cure of their infirmities,
both spiritual and corporal.
I come, therefore, with complete confidence
to implore your maternal intercession for my grandchild.
Obtain, O loving Mother, the grant of my requests *(mention
your specific request here).*
Through gratitude for your favors,
I will endeavor to imitate your virtues, that I may one day share
your glory.
Amen.

ABOUT OUR LADY OF LOURDES

Our Lady appeared to Bernadette Soubirous in Lourdes, France, eighteen times. During the ninth appearance, Our Lady told Bernadette to drink at the fountain and wash herself. Bernadette dug in the mud until she got enough water to clean her face. The next day a spring began to flow, which still flows today. Thousands visit the Lourdes grotto each year to drink the water and bathe there. Many healings have occurred.

Infant of Prague Novena
of Childlike Confidence

O Jesus, who hast said,
"Ask and you shall receive, seek and you shall find,
knock and it will be opened to you,"
through the intercession of Mary, Thy Most Holy Mother,
I knock, I seek, I ask that my prayer be granted. *(Request)*
O Jesus, who hast said,
"All that you ask of the Father in My Name,
he will grant you through the intercession of Mary, Thy Most
   Holy Mother,"
I humbly and urgently ask Thy Father in Thy Name
that my prayer be granted. *(Request)*
O Jesus, who has said,
"Heaven and earth shall pass away but My word shall not pass,"
through the intercession of Mary, Thy Most Holy Mother,
I feel confident that my prayer will be granted. *(Request)*

*Unlike other nine-day novenas, this one is to be said at the same
time every hour for nine consecutive hours—just one day.*

PRAYER TO THE INFANT OF PRAGUE FOR MY GRANDCHILD

Sweet Infant Jesus, many blessings, favors, and miraculous healings
have been attributed to those who honor you.
Hear my prayers for my grandchild, and as always, no matter what I ask,
I know that you will only grant what is good for us.
May your will be done.
Amen.

St. Andrew Novena
(A Prayer to Conceive)

The St. Andrew Novena is often prayed by couples hoping to conceive, but it can be prayed for anything you truly desire in your life or in the life of another. It is a pious belief that those who complete the novena will receive their request. Traditionally, this prayer is said fifteen times each day, from St. Andrew's Feast Day (November 30) to Christmas Eve (December 24).

Hail, and blessed be the hour and moment
in which the Son of God was born
of the most pure Virgin Mary at midnight
in Bethlehem in piercing cold.
In that hour vouchsafe, O my God,
to hear my prayer and grant my desires.
Through the merits of Our Savior, Jesus Christ,
and of his Blessed Mother.
Amen.

Tips for praying the St. Andrew Novena: How do you keep track of how many times you've prayed this novena prayer? It's up to you. Some choose to offer all fifteen prayers at once on each day of the novena; others divide them up—perhaps five times in the morning, five more at noon, and five more before bed. Since St. Andrew's Feast Day falls during Advent, perhaps you could pray your novena while lighting your Advent wreath!

St. Jude Novena
(For Medical Concerns)

This prayer should be offered nine times a day for nine consecutive days.

Most holy apostle, St. Jude, faithful servant and friend of Jesus,
the Church honors and invokes you universally,
as the patron of difficult cases, of things almost despaired of.
Pray for me; I am so helpless and alone.
Intercede with God for me,
that he bring visible and speedy help where help is almost
    despaired of.
Come to my assistance in this great need,
that I may receive the consolation and help of heaven
in all my necessities, tribulations, and sufferings,
particularly—*(mention your specific request here)*—and
that I may praise God with you and all the saints forever.
I promise, O Blessed St. Jude, to be ever mindful
of this great favor granted me by God and
to always honor you as my special and powerful patron, and
to gratefully encourage devotion to you.
Amen.

St. Rita Novena
(For Serious Illness)

This novena should be said for nine consecutive days.

Holy patroness of those in need, St. Rita,
so humble, pure, and patient,
whose pleadings with your divine Spouse are irresistible,
obtain for us from your crucified Jesus our request *(mention
    your specific request here).*
Be favorable toward us for the greater glory of God and your-
    self, and
we promise to honor and sing your praises ever afterward.
Amen.
Pray 3 Hail Marys and 3 Glory Bes

St. Thérèse of the Child Jesus Novena

Whether we realize it or not, many of us view our day by thorns and roses. We think about what was good and what was bad about our day, whom we hurt and whom we helped, what we did well and how we can improve. May our grandchildren be the roses in the lives they encounter. We all need a few thorns to appreciate the roses, but may our grandchildren gather more roses than thorns. May they experience more good days than bad. May they review their days, realize their mistakes, and use them to improve—not just for themselves but for all they encounter.

St. Thérèse, the Little Flower,
please pick for me a rose from the heavenly gardens and send it to me as a message of love.
Ask God to grant the favor I thee implore, and
tell Him I will love Him each day more and more.
Amen.

This prayer plus 5 Our Fathers, 5 Hail Marys, and 5 Glory Bes should be said on five successive days before 11:00 a.m. On the fifth day, the fifth set of prayers having been completed, offer one more set—5 Our Fathers, 5 Hail Marys, and 5 Glory Bes.

Acknowledgments

The author and the publisher wish to express their gratitude to the following for permissions to reproduce or adapt prayers from their publications. The author has made every effort to locate the copyright holder of the secondary source material in this book. Any omissions or changes should be sent to the publisher so that it may be corrected at the next printing. Excerpts have been taken from the following sources:

Pope Francis quotation in the introduction is from Angelus address of Pope Francis in St. Peter's Square on Sunday, July 26, 2015, www.vatican.va.

"For Vocations" quotation is from *A Life For God: The Mother Teresa Reader*, compiled by LaVonne Neff (Ann Arbor, MI: Servant Publications, 1995).

St. Michael Prayer is from Address of Pope John Paul II to the Young People during the Visit at the Sydney Cricket Ground, Sydney, Australia, November 25, 1986, www.vatican.va.

Seven traditional prayers and novenas including "Anima Christi," "St. Teresa's Bookmark," "St. Teresa of Avila Prayer," "Novena to Our Lady of Lourdes," "St. Andrew Novena," "St. Rita Novena," and "St. Therese of the Child Jesus Novena" are from *Catholic Prayers for all Occasions*, ed.

Jacquelyn Lindsey (Huntington, IN: Our Sunday Visitor, 2017), www.osv.com, used by permission.

"The Angelus" is from *Catholic Treasury of Prayers* (Totowa, NJ: Catholic Book Publishing, 2002).

"The Chaplet of Divine Mercy" is from Maria-Faustina Kowalska, *Divine Mercy in My Soul and the Divine Mercy Chaplet* (Stockbridge, MA: Marian Press, 1987), used with permission of the Marian Fathers of the Immaculate Conception of the B.V.M.

"Living Love" quotation is from Francois-Xavier Nguyễn Văn Thuận, *Five Loaves and Two Fish* (Washington, DC: Morley Books, 2000).

"Against Harsh Judgments" quotation is from Francis de Sales, *Introduction to the Devout Life* (New York: Longmans, Green, 1891).

"For Knowing True Beauty" quotation is from *The Letters of St. Catherine of Siena*, translated with an introduction by Suzanne Noffe (Binghampton, NY: Center for Medical and Early Renaissance Studies, 1988).

"In Celebration" quotation is from *Love a Fruit Always in Season: Daily Meditations from the Words of Mother Teresa of Calcutta*, edited by Dorothy S. Hunt (San Francisco: Ignatius Press, 1987).

Five prayers including "Act of Consecration to Our Lady of the Miraculous Medal," "Act of Consecration to the Sacred Heart," "Guardian Angel Prayer," "St. Patrick Breastplate," and "St. Francis Prayer" are from *Manual of Prayers*, fourth printing of the second edition, compiled by Rev. James D. Watkins (published in Illinois by Midwest Theological

Forum, in cooperation with the Pontifical North American College, copyrighted in 1996).

"Mary, Undoer of Knots" is from *Novena Prayer of Our Lady Undoer of Knots*, by Marianne Lorraine Trouve, FSP (Boston: Pauline Books and Media, 2016).

"Infant of Prague Novena of Childlike Confidence" and "St. Jude Novena" are from *Treasured Catholic Prayers*, ed. Bart Tesoriero, (Aquinas Press, Lewisburg, 2018).

"Confirmation" quotation is from *United States Catholic Catechism for Adults* (Washington, DC: USCCB, 2006).

Quotations from "For Faithfulness in Daily Duties" and "For Charity" are from Josemaría Escrivá, *The Way* (New York: Doubleday, 1982).

Julie Dortch Cragon is the co-owner and manager of St. Mary's Bookstore and Church Supply in Nashville, Tennessee. She is the author of a number of books, including *Bless My Child*. She also writes devotions for *Living Faith Kids* magazine.

Cragon earned a bachelor's degree from Vanderbilt University in 1982. She has appeared on EWTN, Sacred Heart Radio, Radio Maria, Relevant Radio, Guadalupe Radio, Mater Dei Radio, Breadbox Media, and Ave Maria Radio.

Cragon lives in Nashville with her husband, Allen. They have six children and one grandchild.

Juliedortchcragon.com
Facebook: Julie Dortch Cragon
Twitter: @juliecragon
Instagram: @juliecragon

AVE

AVE MARIA PRESS

Founded in 1865, Ave Maria Press,
a ministry of the Congregation of
Holy Cross, is a Catholic publishing
company that serves the spiritual and
formative needs of the Church and its
schools, institutions, and ministers;
Christian individuals and families; and
others seeking spiritual nourishment.

For a complete listing of titles from

Ave Maria Press

Sorin Books

Forest of Peace

Christian Classics

visit www.avemariapress.com

AVE | AVE MARIA PRESS
Notre Dame, IN
A Ministry of the United States Province of Holy Cross